# FREE DVD  FREE DVD

## *From Stress to Success* DVD from Trivium Test Prep

Dear Customer,

Thank you for purchasing from Trivium Test Prep! Whether you're a new teacher or looking to advance your career, we're honored to be a part of your journey.

To show our appreciation (and to help you relieve a little of that test-prep stress), we're offering a **FREE** *AP English Literature Essential Test Tips DVD\** by Trivium Test Prep. Our DVD includes 35 test preparation strategies that will help keep you calm and collected before and during your big exam. All we ask is that you email us your feedback and describe your experience with our product. Amazing, awful, or just so-so: we want to hear what you have to say!

To receive your **FREE** *AP English Literature Essential Test Tips DVD*, please email us at 5star@ triviumtestprep.com. Include "Free 5 Star" in the subject line and the following information in your email:

1. The title of the product you purchased.
2. Your rating from 1 – 5 (with 5 being the best).
3. Your feedback about the product, including how our materials helped you meet your goals and ways in which we can improve our products.
4. Your full name and shipping address so we can send your **FREE** *AP English Literature Essential Test Tips DVD*.

If you have any questions or concerns please feel free to contact us directly at 5star@triviumtestprep.com.

Thank you, and good luck with your studies!

\* Please note that the free DVD is not included with this book. To receive the free DVD, please follow the instructions above.

# AP English Literature and Composition Study Guide 2019

## Exam Prep and Practice Test Questions for the AP English Literature and Composition Exam (Guide to 5)

# TABLE OF CONTENTS

# INTRODUCTION

**W**elcome to your complete guide to the AP English Literature exam! This book will provide you with the tips, tricks, and strategies you'll need to do well on the exam. If you've made it this far, you're obviously a student who:

1. Loves English
2. Wants to earn some early college credit
3. Has parents who want you to earn early college credit
4. Is scared to death of the AP exam
5. All of the above

You most likely relate to at least one of those answers. Unfortunately, the questions on the test won't be quite as easy as the above—but there is good news: You can do better on this test than you ever, ever expected.

It may seem like an impossible task: other classes, other AP tests, and a full life outside of school may leave very little time to study. Perhaps you think that you will be lucky simply to pass the test.

Set your sights higher: You don't have to be a prospective English major to perform well on the exam, and you don't even have to be a great English student. The most important aspect to keep in mind is that you must prepare yourself for the test. That doesn't just mean studying—although that doesn't hurt. You need to be as familiar as possible with every single aspect of this test. Think about it: you only have three hours to earn an entire semester's worth of college credit; do you really want to waste those hours cracking the code on directions and what the questions are really asking?

As you might have already noticed, this guide isn't the typical guide to content on the AP Lit exam. You've already seen those and, honestly, what purpose have they served other than re-hashing what your AP Lit teacher is already striving hard to reiterate to you each day? So don't plan on learning how to write a thesis statement again or how to analyze a passage for tone. Instead, this book is going to teach you how to study and prepare for the test: what to study, how to study—the method behind the madness, if you will.

# Achieving AP Success
# with this Book

One thing to remember is that this book—like any study tool, really— is a tool, not a magic bullet. In other words, don't expect to score a 9 on your essay and a 5 composite (the best score possible) merely because you sat down and read the thing from cover to cover. You can use this guide to achieve much greater success on the AP exam than without it, if you remember the following rules:

1. These are tried-and-true tips and techniques: use them.
2. There is a suggested study schedule: stick to it.
3. There are strategies for beating test anxiety: use them.
4. There are practice tests: do them.
5. For those who are keen on seeing that 5, there are even tips for how to elevate your test score: follow them.

So grab some snacks, highlighters, pens, paper, and your English notes. Together, ladies and gentlemen, we are going to knock the AP English Literature Examination out of the park.

# Preparing for the AP English
# Literature Examination

First, let's address a few questions about the test in general; then we can move on to the real work.

**Who takes this test?** Traditionally, students enrolled in the AP English Literature course also take the AP exam; however, you do not need to be enrolled in the course to take the exam.

**What does the test measure?** The AP English Literature exam measures the mastery of skills and abilities regarding the interpretation and evaluation of literature—this means that your ability to understand and evaluate what you are reading is (almost) more important than your content knowledge.

**How do I register for the test?** You will need to register through your high school testing coordinator.

**How much does the test cost?** For students in the United States, U.S. territories, and Canada, the test fee is $89. However, these fees are always subject to change, so consult the College Board website.

**How is the exam structured?** The test is divided into two parts. The first section is a multiple-choice section, which consists of fifty-five questions (on average) about selected passages in prose and poetry. One hour is allotted to complete this portion of the test.

The second section is a free-response section that requires three essays. The first two essays are analytical essays based on included poetry and prose selections. The third essay is an open-ended question, that asks for a response about the most appropriate literary text that you're familiar with. Sometimes a list of titles is included as a source of inspiration; sometimes it's not.

**How long is the test?** The test lasts for three hours: the first hour is for the multiple-choice section and the remaining two hours are dedicated to the essay portion of the exam.

**When do you take the test?** The exam is administered annually in the beginning of May. If you miss the exam for a legitimate reason (as listed below), you may take an alternate form of the test later in May. The College Board does not allow early testing under any circumstances whatsoever.

You won't be charged an additional fee if you miss the test for any of the following excuses that the College Board has deemed legitimate:

- Conflict with International Baccalaureate (IB) exam
- Conflict with state, province, or nationally mandated tests
- Disabilities accommodation issue
- Emergency: bomb scare or fire alarm
- Emergency: serious injury, illness, or family tragedy
- Language lab scheduling conflict
- Religious holiday/observance
- School closing: election, national holiday, or natural disaster
- Strike/labor conflict
- Three or more AP Exams on same date
- Two AP Exams on same date and time

You're charged an extra $45 fee for each AP exam that you miss for the following reasons:

- Academic contest/event
- Athletic contest/event
- Conflict with non-AP and non-IB exam
- Family commitment
- Ordering error
- Other school event
- School closing (local decision, non-emergency)
- If your circumstance differs from any listed above, you must contact AP Services.

**Where do you take the test?** Generally, you take the AP exam at the school where you are enrolled in AP English Literature.

**Why should I take the test?** The main reason you should take the test is that you can earn college credits if you achieve a satisfactory score on the exam. If that's not compelling enough, here are some other reasons why you might decide to go for it:

- You are already enrolled in AP Lit—after all, you've spent an entire year in the class.
- You want to place out of introductory-level English classes in college, although some schools may still require particular courses.
- You can select which colleges sees your scores.

**How is the test scored?** The two sections of the test are scored differently. The multiple-choice section is machine scored and makes up forty-five percent of the total grade. The essay is scored by two AP readers, usually college English professors or AP Literature teachers who have been trained to evaluate student essays according to AP standards. Essays are scored on a scale of 0-9 points.

The total score comes from the multiple-choice section combined with the three essay scores; a final grade of 1-5 comes from this composite score (5 being the highest). A score of 3 indicates that you may be qualified to receive college credit; a score of 4 suggests that you are, indeed, qualified, and a score of 5 shows that you have demonstrated an excellent grasp of the material and are exceedingly qualified to receive college course credit.

In general, colleges will grant credit for scores of 4 or 5 on the test; however, some colleges will accept a 3. Check with the college you'll be attending (or a few that you plan to apply to) and see what AP scores they deem acceptable for course credit.

Keep in mind that you can only earn points on the AP test. You will not be penalized for incorrect answers. What does that mean for you? It's better to make an educated guess—or any guess at all— than to leave an answer blank.

**Will colleges see my scores?** The only colleges that see your exam results are the schools that you hand-select.

**What should I bring with me on test day?** Leave the highlighters, colored pencils, mechanical pencils, dictionary, thesaurus, food, drinks, and cell phone at home. Read that last part again—don't bring your phone, if possible. If you have to, be prepared to give it up for the duration of the exam. Your test proctor may request that all phones be turned off and collect them prior to administering the test.

Bring several already-sharpened pencils with erasers for your multiple choice section, dark blue and black ink pens, and a watch that doesn't beep or have an alarm. Know your social security number (and don't share it with anyone).

If you're home-schooled or testing away from your usual school, make sure you bring your home school code or school code; likewise, if you have received special accommodations from the College Board (that may resemble what you receive in your IEP or 504 plan), bring the College Board SSD Accommodations letter with you.

# What You Can Do to Prepare for the Test

Reading this book is a great first step toward preparing for success on the AP exam, but of course you can do more:

- Reviewing texts, key passages, literary terms and devices and characters, too, are all great ways to get ready for the open-answer essay.
- Pay attention in class, take copious notes, review all of your materials, and consult you teacher for extra advice and guidance when necessary.
- Take advantage of the practice exams included in this guide and any practice exams you receive during class.
- Review all of your answers and pay close attention to those that were incorrect—again, seek guidance from your teacher if you're not sure why your answer was incorrect (or what made the correct answer the right one).
- Don't hesitate to approach another English teacher you may have had once before for extra help: your AP teacher may be the most familiar with the AP testing format, but any English teacher should be able to help you get where you need to go with this test when it comes to content.

Choose two to three different texts you feel comfortable with and prepare them for writing by learning their themes, symbols, details, important passages, and major critical interpretations.

# Study Schedule

Chances are that if you're signed up to take the AP Lit exam, you're probably signed up for a host of other AP exams, too. It can be a super stressful time, no doubt. How can anybody expect you to study for all of those tests when they all happen in the same May window of time? How can you expect yourself to study for all of those tests?

The answer is easier than you think: you have to devise a study schedule. Odds are that you're not just taking the AP test outside of the AP course, so whatever homework you might receive as May approaches can be considered part of your study time—but you also have to dedicate some time for straight-up test prep.

**When should you start?** How about now? Whether you've got one week left before the test or a glorious three months ahead of you, plan to designate at least one hour (preferably more) per week to prepare for your exam. Try to make it the same hour each day—whether that's immediately after school and activities or the hour after dinner, be consistent. Multiple studies have shown that it takes at least 21 days of

The brain can only take in so much new information at once. To effectively study, break your study hour into three twenty-minute chunks and switch topics during each chunk.

repeating the same activity before it becomes an ingrained habit, which is exactly how you want to treat your personal test prep sessions: as a habit.

**Where should you start?** A good starting place will differ from person to person. If you know your biggest area of weakness is writing, start there. Likewise, if you know that you have a hard time determining what a multiple-choice question is really asking, begin by analyzing those questions.

If you have no idea where your weak points are, talk with your AP Lit teacher and see what he or she has to say. Remember not to take this criticism personally since you're asking on purpose in order to find out where you need the most help. If you're still not sure after that point, try taking a few released tests and see how you do—not only will that provide you with a good practice opportunity, it will also guide you towards areas where you need the most improvement.

Everybody has to find a study schedule that fits their needs, but no matter what you decide it's important to set a schedule and stick to it. Below is an example of how you might divide up your week to study for the AP Literature exam:

Monday: Review literary terms and devices

Tuesday: Practice reading essay prompts and writing outlines for those prompts

Wednesday: Take a multiple choice practice test

Thursday: Write a timed essay

Friday: Go over the results from your multiple choice practice test

Saturday: Review authors and novels

By adhering to a study schedule, you're not only focusing your mind on what you're about to be tested on, but you also train yourself to take the test more seriously. You're also less likely to experience the same levels of text anxiety that you may have experienced in the past, since all of this preparation should build your confidence. In essence, you're taking all of the information you've been squirreling away for the winter and airing it out, getting it ready for the spring. You're not re-learning the material; you're learning what you need to do with it.

# We Want to Hear from You

Here at Accepted, Inc. our hope is that we not only taught you the relevant information needed to pass the exam, but that we helped you exceed all previous expectations. Our goal is to keep our guides concise, show you a few test tricks along the way, and ultimately help you succeed in your goals.

On that note, we are always interested in your feedback. To let us know if we've truly prepared you for the exam, please email us at support@acceptedinc.com. Feel free to include your test score!

Your success is our success. Good luck on the exam and your future ventures.

Sincerely,

– The Accepted, Inc. Team –

# PART I: REVIEW

# one

# THE BASICS

## Literary Terms and Devices

One of the most important tasks you need to accomplish for the AP Lit exam is learning literary devices inside and out. You will not understand what the questions are asking if you don't know the devices. Even if they removed the time limit and you rehearsed all of the study strategies in the world, that wouldn't help you make the grade if you don't understand the questions.

If you do nothing else, commit to learning, understanding, and memorizing your literary elements and devices. Do this in whatever way works for you—but avoid cramming. There are numerous reasons why cramming the night before an AP test is a terrible idea, but the most important is this: there are simply too many literary devices. It would be like trying to cook a complete Thanksgiving dinner in a one-hour cooking competition. This is the absolute, number one, must-do-ahead-of-time task. However, this needn't be a dry, dull activity. Some methods for studying include making flash cards and asking friends or family to quiz you; writing a rap or putting the definitions to music and singing them; making a colorful banner and adding a definition card every time you learn and remember one; annotating your favorite poem or story for examples of every single literary device you can think of (or that we list in this book); taking online quizzes daily to remember more terms; making a poster of all the terms you discuss in class on a weekly basis; drawing illustrations or making a collage visually depicting the terms and how they are used; writing a short story personifying the terms and making them speak the way that they are used; for example, Simile would always make comparisons using like or as.

There are eighty terms you need to know for the test. It sounds frightening—eighty terms? But don't worry about memorizing every single one of these terms: the ones that show up most frequently are at the top of the list; however, there's still a chance that the remaining terms and devices may make an appearance on your test. After all, there are roughly one hundred multiple-choice questions heading your way. So learn as many as you can.

You're almost guaranteed to find a question about these terms:

**Allegory**: A figure of speech in which abstract ideas and principles are described in terms of characters, figures and events in order to teach an idea and a principle and deliver a moral lesson.

**Alliteration**: A stylistic literary device identified by the repeated sound of the first consonant in a series of multiple words.

**Ambiguity**: A word, phrase, or statement that contains more than one meaning, leading to vagueness and confusion and shaping the basis for instances of unintentional humor.

**Anecdote**: A short and interesting story or any amusing event often proposed to support or demonstrate some point, usually in order to make the readers laugh or brood over the topic presented.

**Antagonist**: A character or a group of characters who stand in opposition to the protagonist or the main character.

**Connotation**: A cultural and emotional association or meaning implied by a word apart from the literal meaning or denotations that it describes explicitly.

**Diction**: How the author uses word choice to make his or her point. Diction can include the mood, attitude, dialect, and style of the writer's words.

**Emotive language**: The deliberate choice of words to elicit emotion (usually to influence). For instance, the language may be positive or negative or welcoming or threatening, depending on the author's choice of words (see Diction).

**Enjambment**: The continuation of a sentence without a pause beyond the end of a line, couplet, or stanza.

**Epiphany**: Derived from the Greek word *epiphaneia*, epiphany means *appearance* or *manifestation*. In literary terms, an epiphany is that moment in the story where a character achieves realization, awareness or a feeling of knowledge after which events are seen through the prism of this new light in the story.

/' To prepare when learning terms, add examples to your flashcards and practice finding the devices in a passage and then writing down why the author chose it. —/

/' *Diction* is almost certain to appear on the test in conjunction with tone. Practice explaining how word choices influence tone. —/

**Euphemism**: Polite, indirect expressions that replace words and phrases considered harsh and impolite or which suggest something unpleasant.

**Figurative language**: Language that goes beyond literal sensory description by giving a word with a specific meaning, by comparing two things in such a way that you find the comparison interesting or by using words that have unusual constructions or sounds.

**Foreshadowing**: Plot events that hint at what is to come later in the story.

**Hyperbole**: An exaggeration of ideas for the sake of emphasis; from the Greek word meaning "over-casting."

**Imagery**: Descriptive language that represents objects, actions and ideas by appealing directly to physical senses.

**Irony**: The expression of the opposite of expectation in terms of idea, language, or event, typically for humorous or emphatic effect.

**Metaphor**: A comparison between two unlike things for rhetorical effect or to highlight the similarities between the two.

**Narrator**: A personal character or a non-personal voice developed to deliver information to the audience. The narrator may be an anonymous voice, the author himself, or another fictional or nonfictional character in the story.

**Ode**: Originally from a Greek word meaning *to sing or chant*, the ode is a poetic form with a long history and varied character. In modern use, typically a form of lyrical poetry that expresses strong emotion addressed to an object or entity not present.

**Paradox**: From the Greek word *paradoxon* that means *contrary to expectations, existing belief or perceived opinion*. It is a statement that appears to be self-contradictory or outlandish but may include a hidden truth. It is also used to illustrate an opinion or statement contrary to accepted traditional ideas.

**Parody**: Parody is an imitation of a particular writer, artist or a genre, exaggerating it deliberately to produce a comic effect.

**Personification**: A figure of speech in which a thing, an idea or an animal is given human attributes and seem to have the ability to act like a human being.

**Protagonist**: The central character or leading figure in poetry, narrative, novel or any other story, sometimes called a *hero* by the audience.

**Satire**: A technique in which writers adopt a specific persona that uses humor, irony, exaggeration and ridicule to expose and criticize foolishness and corruption of an individual or a society.

**Simile**: A figure of speech that makes a comparison between two different things by using the words *like* or *as*.

**Sonnet**: A poetic form consisting of fourteen lines written in iambic pentameter (ten syllables per line in a rhythmic pattern of unstressed and stressed syllables). Sonnets have specific rhyme schemes.

**Style**: The specific techniques that an individual author uses, depending upon one's syntax, word choice, and tone.

**Symbolism**: Assigning metaphoric or abstract meaning, different from the literal sense, to specific objects or entities. Often, a specific object or entity will take on a consistent meaning or idea throughout the text.

**Syntax**: The specific structure, order, and type of sentences in a text that spring from the rules of a language; the way that different parts of speech are put together in order to convey a complete thought.

**Tone**: The writer's attitude or emotion toward a subject, generally conveyed through the author's choice of words.

The remaining terms may not be as popular, but don't disregard them:

Practice for the test by looking for examples of these literary devices in your reading.

- anaphora
- anti-climatic
- apostrophe
- assonance
- blank verse
- climax
- colloquial language
- convention
- consonance
- couplet
- deus ex machina
- denouement
- doppelganger
- elegy
- epic hero
- epilogue
- epistolary
- euphony
- expansion
- fable
- flashback
- flat character
- foil
- folklore
- free verse
- genre
- gothic novel
- hubris

- illocution
- in medias res
- inversion
- memoir
- meter
- metonymy
- motif
- neutral language
- onomatopoeia
- poetic justice
- prequel
- prologue
- prose
- pun
- rhyme scheme
- rising action
- rite of passage
- round character
- resolution
- slang
- soliloquy
- tragedy

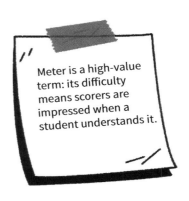

Meter is a high-value term: its difficulty means scorers are impressed when a student understands it.

### HOW TO REVIEW LITERARY TERMS

There are several steps to making sure you have a firm understanding of literary terms before taking the AP Literature exam. First, make sure you have a complete understanding of the top thirty terms—these are the ones you'll find on both sections of the exam and probably be expected to write about. To do this, investigate any term you know you've heard but don't quite understand or need an example for. Next, work on familiarizing yourself with terms you haven't heard before so that they're not completely foreign to you on test day. During both of these steps, make flash cards to use for self-study or in a group study session where you can also discuss examples from class or outside reading.

## Important Authors

You'll need to be prepared to discuss specific works in-depth on the open-ended essay question, and of course you'll see works by many important authors throughout the rest of the exam. While there's no way to know exactly which texts will show up, it's good to familiarize yourself with important novelists and poets. There's no required reading list from the College Board (although your AP English teacher might have other ideas for you); however, the Board does provide a list of novelists you may want to consider for test preparation:

- Isabel Allende
- Rudolfo Anaya
- Margaret Atwood
- Jane Austen
- James Baldwin
- Saul Bellow
- Charlotte Brontë
- Emily Brontë
- Willa Cather
- Sandra Cisneros
- Kate Chopin
- Joseph Conrad
- Daniel Defoe
- Charles Dickens
- Fyodor Dostoevsky
- George Eliot

- Ralph Ellison
- Louise Erdrich
- William Faulkner
- F. Scott Fitzgerald
- Thomas Hardy
- Nathaniel Hawthorne
- Ernest Hemingway
- Zora Neale Hurston
- Henry James
- James Joyce
- D. H. Lawrence
- Bernard Malamud
- Gabriel García Márquez
- Cormac McCarthy
- Herman Melville
- Toni Morrison
- Bharati Mukherjee
- Flannery O'Connor
- Jonathan Swift
- Mark Twain
- John Updike
- Alice Walker
- Eudora Welty
- Edith Wharton
- Virginia Woolf
- Richard Wright

Keep in mind that nonfiction selections may appear on the AP Literature Exam and while these passages will not be subjected to the same line of questioning that accompanies the AP Language Exam, you will need to analyze and investigate their use of literary devices in the same way that you would for novel, drama, and short story passages.

While many students feel that the main difference between AP Literature and AP Language can be broken down into fiction vs. nonfiction, that doesn't mean that non-fiction pieces are confined solely to the AP Language test. On the contrary, the College Board site recommends the following non-fiction writers to review, as their work may possibly appear on the AP Lit test:

- Joseph Addison
- Matthew Arnold
- James Baldwin
- Jesús Colón
- Joan Didion
- Frederick Douglass
- W. E. B. Du Bois
- Ralph Waldo Emerson
- Michael Pollan
- David Thoreau
- E. B. White

# Annotations

If you enrolled in pre-AP classes prior to taking any AP English, you've been annotating for a long time. The good news is that you can put all of that annotation training to work on this test.

Don't go overboard. The first item to bear in mind is not to get annotation-happy—if you write too much and highlight everything, you may lose the point of what you were noticing to begin with, or you may use up too much time. On your practice tests, make quick marks on passages during the first reading—words that stick out to you, unfamiliar vocabulary, literary elements such as imagery, similes, metaphors, or other literary devices the author may have used.

Practice annotations ahead of time. If you are already in the practice of reading passages with a pencil in hand, then you don't have too much to worry about: reading texts and scanning for clues is second-nature to you now. However, if the idea of marking up a text as you read along is still new to you, start reading with a pen in hand.

Time is of the essence. You don't want to get hung up on annotating "correctly," as many students do who are accustomed to submitting annotations of class texts to their teachers. Remember that although your teacher is checking to see if you noted specific items, they're doing this so that you get used to the practice of close reading. Nobody will be checking your test booklet to see if you annotated "correctly." Therefore, it's in your best interest to make note of what really captures your attention about a text during the first read (since you will usually only have one chance to read through the passage in the limited time frame of the test).

Remember the acronym DIDLS while annotating: Diction, Imagery, Details, Language, Syntax. This will help you focus on all important text elements while you read.

# two

# WRITING THE ESSAY

Although the essay section is the second part of the AP Lit exam, this is the part of the test that everyone worries about the most (which makes sense; after all, you're responsible for generating all of your own ideas and answers here, since there aren't any guesses to make or any bubbles to fill in) so this is where we start.

Remember, the essay section consists of three essays—two analytical and one open-ended response. If you are enrolled in the course, there will certainly be one or more texts you recognize on the open-answer section. If not, that's ok, too—the list of suggested texts are merely suggestions so you don't have to rack your brain thinking of titles. However, if a few well-known pieces of literature come to mind and you know enough about them to craft an elegant, concise essay, by all means, use them.

To that end, the most important suggestion to keep in mind, even if you somehow forget to follow all of the others, is this: you have control over this. The entire point of this essay is to formulate a thesis and defend it. Remember, all you have to do is communicate your own ideas about how things are similar or dissimilar along with a working knowledge of the literary terms and devices in question, and if you've survived a year of AP Lit thus far, you can surely do this. It's a matter of belief in yourself and your own ideas. You'll be in the clear as long as you answer the question and defend your assertions well.

We all can agree that being prepared never hurt; it can only enhance your final performance. Practice makes perfect, right? While you'll have ample opportunities to practice on mock exams later on, there are several other techniques you can practice that will make writing these essays easier and that will improve your writing overall.

You can choose which essay to start first. Choose the one you feel most comfortable writing so that you have at least one good essay score under your belt.

# Step One: Practice Reading the Prompt

This may sound silly to you. After all, as a high school student preparing to take an AP Literature exam, you no doubt have ample experience with reading essay test prompts; it's actually not silly at all, though. Imagine the following hypothetical situation: it's test day, you're finally at the open-answer essay, and you blaze through with a few minutes to spare. You're proud of yourself: you incorporated quotations, elaborated, analyzed, and you think you've just knocked the socks off of your essay's future AP reader. You decide to look over your essay once more before closing the booklet—just to edit for spelling and grammar—and you notice that you didn't address what the prompt was asking—at all.

The sad truth is that this hypothetical situation isn't fictional. Students frequently catch hold of one aspect of what the prompt demands and run with it, neglecting the other portion of the prompt or even taking the essay into an entirely different direction than the one the prompt asks for.

Spend an extra sixty seconds reviewing each prompt. Underline or circle any ideas that repeat themselves—these are the key concepts that the essay needs to address. Find the main task given to you by the prompt by circling any verbs you see. Number the different elements that the prompt expects you to include in your essay. In fact, feel free to go ahead and mark the prompt up just the way you've been doing all year with close reading and annotations—this is not different. After crafting a thesis, consider returning to the prompt to double-check that you have addressed every required element.

By understanding what is being asked of you, you can deliver the proper goods.

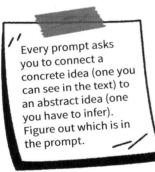

Every prompt asks you to connect a concrete idea (one you can see in the text) to an abstract idea (one you have to infer). Figure out which is in the prompt.

# Step Two: Practice Writing Outlines

A common problem with student essays is poor writing thanks to a lack of structure and organization. Often, students with excellent ideas feel pressed for time; they let the ticking clock get the best of them and wind up churning out as many ideas as they can in a short amount of time. While this may not sound so bad, the poison lies in the failure to elaborate and make connections with previously made points of argument. Many times, it is better to make fewer points but elaborate on each one with more clarity and depth.

Combat organizational issues by practicing with outlines. Find sample writing prompts from the College Board online (or from your

AP teacher). Set a timer for four minutes and go through steps to help you get the important information from each prompt quickly and correctly. First, read the prompt. Then read the prompt again, and maybe even one more time for good measure; think like a mathematician and solve this equation: what is my essay going to be about? Use a simple outline format to help guide your ideas:

> A: Introduction and thesis statement
>
> B: Body Paragraphs
>
> C: Conclusion

Did the timer go off while you were still on the first step? That's ok—try again. The point is to learn a new method that you can actually apply to the test itself. It's much better to figure out that you're spending too much time formulating an outline when you're studying at home than when you're taking the test in May.

The benefits to this study technique are innumerable, but surely you can see that by rehearsing outlines you'll be able to formulate a plan of attack on that open-answer essay in minutes. Plus, by reviewing loads of prompts and writing just as many outlines, you become familiar with a wide variety of questions that might be included in your actual prompt.

While you should begin practicing this technique with the open-ended response essay prompts, because you are already familiar with the text you will use to support your argument, you can also apply this method to the analysis essay prompts by adding in time to read and analyze the passage. Remember that the suggested time for each essay is only forty minutes—you probably don't want to spend more than ten of those on reading the prompt and passage and formulating your outline.

If you find yourself pressed for time, write your outline on the answer booklet itself and just leave space for elaboration. You will get some credit for the direction your ideas are taking and the organization, even if you do not finish elaborating.

## Step Three: Practice Writing Introductions

Another major complaint from the AP Readers is this: *students don't know how to write an introduction.* There are many students who still struggle with crafting an introduction, and the AP Lit essays have their own specific demands for an introduction. When it comes to writing an introduction for any of your three AP exam essays, there are several things to keep in mind. Do not under any circumstances summarize the prompt, begin with a general statement, offer quotations or statistics that aren't specifically contained in the exam text, or forget to address what the prompt asks!

On the other hand, there are several things you will always want to make sure to do in your introduction. First of all, begin with a thesis statement so that the readers will immediately understand what you mean to say. Be sure to include the author's name(s) and title of the work(s) in your thesis statement and to specifically address whatever the prompt is asking regarding literary devices, interpretations, and tone. Keep your emphasis on the selection you're being tested on. Finally, specifically address what the prompt asks from the get-go and do not stray from it.

## How To Practice

Set a timer for five minutes. Once you've fully read through and dissected your prompt, formulate a mental response—consider the parallels you're being asked to draw between the two texts (or two ideas, devices, et cetera) and write your findings clearly and succinctly—don't try to impress the AP Readers with your million-dollar SAT words if you're not one hundred percent positive you're using them correctly! Be sure to include author names and titles of texts.

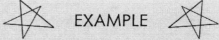 **EXAMPLE**

Consider this sample prompt, which is based on a passage from Shakespeare's *Othello*: Discuss how Shakespeare's characterization of Iago reveals the character's true motives in this passage from the tragedy *Othello*.

Consider what Student A wrote:

*Shakespeare uses indirect characterization to reveal Iago's true motives in Othello. This paper will demonstrate just how Shakespeare accomplishes this.*

While this imaginary student did indeed create a thesis statement, use the author's name and title of the work, and even avoided a form of the verb *to be*, he or she wasted time! The student merely rephrased the prompt rather than answering it.

Now, look at Student B's answer. Notice the parts that are the same and the parts that are more specific:

*In this passage, Shakespeare reveals how Iago's all-consuming jealousy compels his behavior through the use of speech and physical action.*

This imaginary student came right out and identified Iago as a jealous character and listed two methods of indirect characterization (speech, action). The reader now knows what the rest of the essay will focus on.

If you struggle to write introductions without rephrasing the question, it's time to practice getting over that. There are some key steps you can take to practice writing direct, specific thesis statements and introductions, rather than vague, ambiguous restatements of the prompt. To begin practicing, re-write a prompt just the way Student A did in the example above. Highlight the key words that the prompt wants you to address; in the case of Student A, the key words are *characterization* and *Iago's true motives* (or what those traits revealed). Separate those key words and think about them in terms of how they relate to the passage. Specify how the author used those key terms and what it meant; in the sample about Iago, Shakespeare used speech and action, or indirect characterizations, to show how jealousy was the source of the Iago's behavior. Student B mentions all of these things directly and clearly. Once you have determined the answer for your own sample prompt, substitute that answer for any unclear references in your original statement.

# Considering Audience

When you're writing a paper for class, you might have a tendency to gear your writing towards your teacher; for example, you know that he or she loves to see a favorite vocabulary word or particular concept addressed in an essay, so you make sure to include it. Likewise, you understand what he or she despises seeing in a paper, so you make sure to leave that out. Some of your teacher's preferences are based on their knowledge of what constitutes good writing, while others stem from personal taste. Like it or not, that's writing.

On the writing portion of the exam, you're not writing for your specific AP teacher—and you're not writing to a specific AP Reader, either, so don't try to cater to some hypothetical preferences. Instead, try to write for the general reader, because that is how your AP Reader has been trained to view the paper.

Who's the general reader? Any person of general intelligence who possesses a decent educational background and who pays attention to both the world around them and the world at large.

Since you now understand that you're writing with an imaginary general reader in mind, you should feel even more compelled to write succinctly and accessibly; that is, don't drop million-dollar words if you can send your message in a more direct way (and especially don't try to use any terms unless you are confident you can use the terms correctly—otherwise you'll make a fool out of yourself).

In his essay Politics and the English Language, the great English writer, George Orwell, laid out his six rules for writing. Orwell, like all writers, broke his own rules (and often) but in general, he used these as a framework. You may also find them useful.

1.  Never use a metaphor, simile, or other figure of speech which you are used to seeing in print (essentially, avoid clichés).
2.  Never use a long word where a short one will do.
3.  If it is possible to cut a word out, always cut it out.
4.  Never use the passive where you can use the active.

5. Never use a foreign phrase, a scientific word, or a jargon word if you can think of an everyday English equivalent.

6. Break any of these rules sooner than say anything outright barbarous.

# Essay-Writing Tips

Remember these general tips for writing success as well. They are based on typical mistakes students make when writing an essay like the AP Literature exam essays.

**Do not summarize the plot!** Most AP readers agree that this is one of the very worst things you can do on any of your essays—unless you're trying to get a 1. Here's why: when you summarize, all you're really doing is spitting back information into your own words. You're not bringing any new thoughts to the table. The essay is all about new thoughts—your thoughts on how an author is using hyperbole to create a larger statement, how he creates symbolism through imagery, and so forth.

**Include relevant quotations from the text to support your ideas.** Failing to include direct examples from the text results in a lower score.

**Explain why you included those quotes.** Elaborate on those quotations by explaining how the ones you chose perfectly demonstrate your original point. Respond to those quotations the same way you should respond directly to the prompt. A good rule of thumb to follow: you should always have at least three times as much to say about the quote than the quote itself.

**It's not about you.** This is analytical writing about the text itself—no matter how tempting it may be to show the reader how you can personally relate, keep yourself out of it. That includes whether you like or dislike the text given! The AP Readers want to see your analysis, not whether you found the passage boring, interesting, well-written, or confusing.

**Don't write one giant paragraph and call it an essay.** No matter what—no matter how pressed for time you feel or how tired you might be from studying the night before (more on that later)—do not submit one giant paragraph. Divide your thoughts into paragraphs and use clear transitions.

**Don't over quote.** Don't use so many quotations that your paper becomes a look-alike for the passage itself: you need to prove that you can take the passage and say something intelligent about it, draw inferences from it, see the bigger picture. Similarly, do not use a quotation as a topic sentence. Quotations are meant to support your ideas—your topic sentences should state those ideas clearly.

**Write neatly.** Remember that the Reader has to be able to understand what you wrote in order to evaluate it. It's sad but true: if you

Creating an outline first can help determine where to begin new paragraphs. If you find you have written one big paragraph, though, use the *indent* proofreading symbol (¶) to indicate where the paragraph starts. Readers will give you credit for that; of course, it is better to do it correctly the first time!

write with a sloppy hand, you risk having your work glossed over by a tired Reader who may have lost interest. Take pride in your work and do your best to keep it neat; it shows you care.

If you know you have messy handwriting, practice writing neatly—and quickly—as part of your study routine.

**Review your work (if time allows).** Do you have time left on the clock? Good—go back to the prompt and compare the question to the answer you've written down, making sure that you have included all the necessary keywords in your thesis. This is where it gets tricky: you don't want to replicate, paraphrase, or summarize the thesis. Only reiterate the key literary terms, devices, periods, and so forth that you are being asked to analyze—this will keep you on track.

**Proofread.** Be sure to proofread for grammar and spelling errors! If you make a mistake in your essay, just draw a simple line through it—don't go crazy scribbling over and muddying up your paper. Readers know that the essay isn't going to be the shiny diamond in a platinum setting, but do your best to keep things neat when it comes to your handwriting and your use of the English language.

**Avoid clichés.** If you want to bring your score from a 2 to a 3, a 3 to a 4, or a 4 to a 5 (and who doesn't want to do that?), you must avoid clichés at all costs. By using original phrases and language, your writing will be stronger, which will bump it to the next level. Now, if you feel like you're not clever enough or creative enough to come up with a new way of saying something, well, first, you need to amp up your confidence and self-esteem because you surely can have your own way of saying things. Next, consider how you can change a cliché by addressing specific points from the text or example, instead of just using the broad idea. Include some details or change the words based on the example you want to discuss. For example, instead of saying "time heals all wounds," say something like "as time passes, we can examine emotional wounds and begin to understand and heal them." Same idea, same message, just rephrased to address the situation. The key to rephrasing a cliché is to be specific about the idea and context.

**Avoid vague language.** Your essay will suffer if you rely on words and phrases that do not clearly describe your ideas or that have been used so many times that they have lost meaning. If you feel like something is *beautiful*, *scenic*, or *vivid*, consider what makes it look that way, and talk about that instead of just using a bland, subjective adjective.

**Don't just restate your thesis upon concluding.** While you shouldn't go introducing brand-new ideas at the end of an already-established essay, you might want to consider how your thesis statement connects to the world at large and use that as a way to conclude your essay instead of merely paraphrasing your thesis statement.

**Mix up your sentences.** A slew of sentences strung together the same way isn't very interesting to read and isn't very sophisticated at all. Vary your sentence structure to impress your AP Reader and to demonstrate

Learn to use two to three "special" sentence structures really well and then use them in your essay intentionally. Make sure they fit, though—a fancy sentence where a simple one fits better will not impress anyone.

that not only do you have sophisticated thoughts about literature but that you can also write about them in a sophisticated way.

**Don't be passive.** Always use active voice when you can—it shows a stronger grasp of language usage since you're making the verbs do their job.

**Don't assume you have to stick to the traditional five-paragraph essay.** Your AP Reader doesn't have the time to count your paragraphs—and he or she may not actually notice how many you have (unless you make the mistake of submitting one big paragraph). Say what you have to say in an organized way and don't spend time worrying about how many paragraphs you've written: some students submit three, others seven.

**Length is not a necessary requirement.** Again, it's not about how long or short your essay is (although an incredibly brief paragraph submitted as your essay will most likely be discounted). Don't use filler material to make your essay seem longer; readers are impressed by the quality of your writing and your ability to formulate ideas and defend them. Once again, the quality of the work, not the quantity, is what matters.

# three

# THE OPEN-ENDED QUESTION

The primary misconceptions about the open-ended question is that you must use one of the texts provided to you and that this is the hardest part of the literature exam. In reality, neither of those things is true. When you have the chance to write an essay, you are in complete control; you are in the driver's seat. You even get to choose if you're driving a Maserati or the beat-up family station wagon. In fact, this is the first time on the test that you are the complete, total, original author.

Yes, you just completed two other essays, but you were required to address specific items about specific, assigned passages. On the open-answer question, you get to choose which text(s) to write about. Usually, test-takers are provided with a list of suggested titles that they may want to choose from to complete the open-answer question. Students tend to panic, thinking things like I've only read a few of these titles and I barely remember the plot, let alone the characters. However, it states very clearly that you may use one of the suggested novels or a piece of equal or substantial literary merit (more on that in a moment).

When you complete this portion of the exam, the most important idea to keep in mind is to address the prompt specifically and in as detailed a fashion as you can muster in the short amount of time allotted to this task.

## Study Tool: Card Reports

Simply stated, a card report is a summary book report that can fit on an index card. If you are reading this book early in the school year, you can begin making card reports right away, beginning with the first assigned reading. If you're reading this book closer to May, then follow the tips below.

Why bother creating a card report if you've already analyzed, discussed, and written about the text in class? Here's why: because you can only remember so many details of potential AP open-answer novels. Writing a short card report will not only help you recall those details, but it will assist you in preparing specific pieces for your open-answer discussion.

Even though it's not incredibly detailed, having the following key elements of the card report will be helpful come crunch-time: title, author, characters, themes, symbols, brief plot summary, key quotations from the text, questions for discussion (either from class or self-generated), and possible opening lines or thesis statements you could use.

Since you ought to have your own literary arsenal ready for the open-answer/open-question portion of the exam, prepare at least seven to ten card reports so that you can write at length about those texts. Some smart choices would include:

- Shakespearean tragedy
- Shakespearean comedy
- world literature piece
- satire or allegory
- comedy of manners, or piece about society
- rite of passage
- a piece about death and/or loss
- a piece about love and/or relationships
- a piece about identity
- a piece about morality

When in doubt, remember that you can really never go wrong with Shakespeare. Most of Shakespeare's plays fit into one (or all) of the categories listed above and feature a vast cast that allows for more characters to compare and contrast against each other. The playwright's greatest works all contain numerous subplots from which you may draw various potential themes and motifs: Man versus man, nature, the world—all are contained in Shakespeare. In addition, the man was a master of puns and language usage, so if you're keen on that sort of thing and you can speak to it eloquently, you can put that to use in your essay.

The following are recommended titles:

- tragedies: *Othello, Hamlet*
- comedies: *A Midsummer Night's Dream, Much Ado About Nothing*
- world literature: *Oedipus Rex, Antigone*
- satire: *Gulliver's Travels, 1984*
- allegory: *Animal Farm, Lord of the Flies*
- society: *The Importance of Being Earnest, Pride and Prejudice, The Scarlet Letter, A Tale of Two Cities*

Choose a few texts that can fit into multiple categories. Then, make sure you know those texts best of all come test day. It will be easier to apply one of them to the prompt because they fit so many ideas and perspectives.

- death/loss: *A Separate Peace*, *Death of a Salesman*
- love/relationships: *Romeo and Juliet*, *King Lear*, *Emma*
- beauty: *Pygmalion*, *The Picture of Dorian Gray*
- morality: *Jane Eyre*, *The Crucible*

# Writing Hacks For The Open-Answer Question

So what's the best way to put all of your preparation to use? Try these simple tactics:

**Differentiate.** Try to formulate a list of titles that are as different as possible (in style and genre) from the main work you're preparing for the test. Why? If you can write eloquently about the similarities between the pieces, you're demonstrating to the AP Reader that you have a higher level of thinking than most. For instance, it's natural to compare *The Scarlet Letter* and *The Crucible*: they're both from the same time period and cover a similar sense of morality (or lack thereof, depending on how you look at it). But what would it be like to compare *The Scarlet Letter* to *Macbeth* or *Julius Caesar*? Better yet, how about *The Scarlet Letter* and *The Importance of Being Earnest*? You have a Nathaniel Hawthorne novel contrasted against an Oscar Wilde play—different settings, styles, and plots—but what do the two share? That would make for a highly interesting essay that would do nothing more than compel a reader to reward you highly (provided you write concisely and defend your points adequately).

**Practice paragraphs.** To gain even more practice with writing and preparing a piece for the open-answer question, try using your prepared pieces to write a practice introduction paragraph. Look up writing prompts online and see which of your prepared pieces can best address the question of the prompt. Better yet, set a timer and see if you can write your sample paragraph under similar test conditions.

**Get specific.** The more specific your writing and the clearer your message, the easier it is for the reader to understand. Make sure you use plenty of specific nouns, active verbs, and appropriate adjectives (don't get too slaphappy on the adjectives, but don't be anemic with them, either).

# Practice Prompts

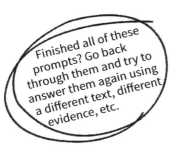
Finished all of these prompts? Go back through them and try to answer them again using a different text, different evidence, etc.

Try your prepared pieces against these prompts from previous years:

1. From a novel or play, choose a character (not necessarily the protagonist) whose mind is pulled in conflicting directions by two compelling desires, ambitions, obligations, or influences. Then, in a well-organized essay, identify each

of the two conflicting forces and explain how this conflict with one character illuminates the meaning of the work as a whole.

2. Choose a novel or play in which one or more of the characters confront a mystery. Then write an essay in which you identify the mystery and explain how the investigation illuminates the meaning of the work as a whole. Do not merely summarize the plot.

3. Select a novel or play in which a character's apparent madness or irrational behavior plays an important role. Then write a well-organized essay in which you explain what this delusion or eccentric behavior consists of and how it might be judged reasonable. Explain the significance of the *madness* to the work as a whole. Do not merely summarize the plot.

4. Choose a novel or play in which a morally ambiguous character plays a pivotal role. Then write an essay in which you explain how the character can be viewed as morally ambiguous and why his or her moral ambiguity is significant to the work as a whole. Avoid mere plot summary.

5. Choose a novel or play of literary merit that requires a character to keep a secret. In a well-organized essay, briefly explain the necessity for secrecy and how the character's choice to reveal or keep the secret affects the plot and contributes to the meaning of the work as a whole. You may select a work from the list below, or you may choose another work of recognized literary merit suitable to the topic. Do NOT write about a short story, poem, or film.

# Still Worried?

Still have questions about the open-ended essay? Here's a few more tips to alleviate your test-day anxiety.

**What if I don't finish my essay?** Don't sweat it, really. The AP readers have been trained to reward students who do what they do well, not what they don't get to. If you have an excellent introduction and a well-developed paragraph or two that fully demonstrates your points, then you'll probably be okay. You will most definitely get credit for the written work that you submit. The only sure-fire way to earn zero points is to submit a blank page.

**What do I do if I can't write about any of the books on the suggested titles list?** First, make sure that you know what the question is asking. Consider the titles that you prepared for this very instance and try to develop your essay around the titles that best address the topic in the prompt.

**Should I choose a work from the list or another work that I know better?** In this instance, the choice is up to you. Actually, the choice is up to the prompt: which work will you be able to use that can answer the prompt's question in the best way? Maybe you don't know one of the suggested titles inside and out, but what you do know about it can contribute an awful lot to your essay—go with it. Likewise, the strongest title that you've prepared may not be able to address the prompt in any way, shape, or form (unless you've prepared a Shakespearean play, in which case you might be all right, since Shakespeare's works contain a wealth of characters and subplots from which to draw for this essay).

**What if the Reader doesn't recognize the work I choose?** In case you're still worried that the reader might not have read the work you reference, stop worrying: it's impossible for every human (AP readers included) to have read and memorized every possible book that a student might refer to on his or her open-answer essay. If the reader isn't familiar with the work you chose to discuss, he or she will just pass it on to another reader who is familiar with it. Just make sure you've thoroughly and precisely addressed the question, regardless of which novel, play, or novella you choose to use.

# four

# THE MULTIPLE-CHOICE SECTION

Studying for the multiple choice section of the AP Lit exam is much like studying for the multiple choice section of any standardized test. This can mean two different things to two different kinds of students. See which category you fall into:

Category One: The Tests-Are-Easy-For-Me-Semi-Slacker Student. So if you're the kind of person who might be a bit lazy in class but performs sky-high on state-mandated tests and things like the SAT and ACT (I know you're out there), congratulations! I'm not going to promise that you'll ace this section, but you'll probably come close. Statistically, if you've done well on tests formatted this way in the past, there's a good chance you'll do well on this one, too. Here's a helpful hint, though: you don't get a pass-go-collect-two-hundred-dollars for this section, because even the best test takers can always stand to do better than they did before.

Category Two: The I-Make-The-Honor-Roll-But-Stink-At-These-Tests Student. You work hard, do your best, and make the honor roll, but your test scores just don't seem to line up with your report cards… and this really bothers you. Rest assured that this doesn't mean any slight towards your intelligence or abilities. Possibly, you suffer from one or more of the following issues:

- You psych yourself out over the test.
- You over-think the questions.
- You worry about time, creating more anxiety.
- You keep thinking every question is a trick question (which it's not).
- You read the directions, the question, or the prompt incorrectly.
- Some other testing anxiety or pitfall.

You can benefit greatly from the tips and practice tests in this book. Read on to learn how to succeed at the multiple-choice section.

# Multiple-Choice Passages

During this portion of the exam, you will answer somewhere between fifty and sixty questions about literature. The texts and questions are both indicative of the college-level work you've been doing this year as well as the college-level work you're trying to obtain credit for.

Passages are comprised of complete poems and excerpts from fiction, drama, and non-fiction. While it's common to see an AP Lit exam filled with nothing but poetry and fiction, do note that other kinds of literature may make an appearance on the test.

Test writers typically try to include at least one early American or European writing, one modern one, and one poem.

Fortunately, you will not be subjected to an exam made entirely of early American writers or Shakespearean sonnets; the test attempts to include readings from a variety of places and eras in literature. You'll also be given background information regarding the passage, usually indicating the author, time period, the larger body of work it may come from, and other pertinent facts. Pay attention to these; the makers of the test didn't arbitrarily include these details— they may come up again in one of the test questions.

# Types of Questions

You probably wonder what sorts of information the test may ask you about prose and poetry. While you ought to prepare several novels to address the open question, you can't really study particular poems or short stories for the multiple-choice section since the questions will be about elements of the passages—this isn't a factual-recall type of test.

To study for this type of test, identify important passages in the work and practice annotating it for literary devices and meaning.

Poetry questions will be about:

- dramatic situation
- structure
- theme
- grammar
- diction

- vocabulary or word meanings in context
- images and figurative language
- tone, literary devices, and metrics

Prose questions will be about:

- situation (plot) and content
- meaning of words or phrases in context
- grammar

- diction
- figurative language
- structure
- literary techniques
- tone

Do you notice any overlapping ideas here? You should. Since poets, playwrights, journalists, and novelists share the same literary toolbox, it's in your best interest to make sure you know and understand the elements of literature inside and out.

# Multiple Choice Tips

### TIP ONE: SCAN THE PASSAGES

You can actually use the time constraints of the test to your advantage on the multiple-choice section. It may seem counterintuitive, but it makes sense: because you have less time to take the test, you have less time to read the passages, which means you need to work on the *Three Ss*: Skimming, Scanning, and Summarizing.

When you skim the passage, you're noting how long it is. When you scan the passage, it's like putting the passage through a scanning device that briefly sees the whole picture (but doesn't spend an inordinate amount of time looking over it). Summarizing is the key to comprehending the piece quickly—and this is also where many students stumble. The key to summarizing is not to do it at the very end of a text; instead, summarize the passage to yourself in small portions while you're scanning.

The best way to maximize the power of the *Three Ss* is to annotate while you're scanning and summarizing—circling words, underlining imagery, jotting a comment in the margin—all of these tools combine to produce a working understanding of the text in question.

Again, set a timer for yourself—you might get sick of doing it, but every time you set that timer, think of yourself like an Olympian preparing for the games and trying to beat the clock. Set about three minutes for the sole purpose of skimming, scanning, and summarizing a passage. See if you can get through it, make some notes, and move towards the questions within the limit that you've set.

### TIP TWO: ANNOTATE THE QUESTIONS

The AP test is hard, for sure, but the one grace you receive in this multiple-choice section is the phrasing of the questions. By noting key words and trigger words, you can decipher what the question is really asking of you and do a better job of decoding the questions. One way to do this is by actually annotating the questions.

The number one reason students fail to answer a multiple-choice questions correctly is because they simply didn't know the right answer. The number two reason is because they didn't understand what the question was asking.

Have you ever gotten a test back from a teacher, gone over the answers in class, and realized: *Oh, THAT'S what she meant by that!* Or

The *EXCEPT* question: For this tricky question, circle *EXCEPT* so you remember that you are looking for the wrong answer, not the right one! Be sure to cross out the letter choices that have right answers—making them wrong!—so you do not accidentally pick them.

thought the question was asking the opposite? In order to avoid this testing pitfall, concentrate on discovering what each question is actually asking. Be careful not to read through questions so quickly that you miss important information.

The AP English Literature exam will never, ever ask you to simply identify a fact contained in the text—recall is not considered a higher-level thinking skill and therefore has no place on this exam. Generally, the exam contains questions of a higher caliber of difficulty than the usual chapter or unit test in school, which means you have to be even more careful about reading and understanding the questions correctly. Annotation will help you do that.

### TIP THREE: LEARNING TO DECODE QUESTIONS

Sometimes it feels like the test would be easy if the test writers would just write in plain English. Actually, the questions are written in a very concise fashion; that is, they are asking you about a certain, precise, direct aspect of the passage in question. Even if the phrasing sounds ornamental, it is actually very concise and purposeful. Each question uses common trigger phrases to help categorize the question and show test-takers what type of question it is.

The more practice you have decoding the questions, the better you'll be able to sail through this section of the test. Look for the following trigger words and terms:

*According to the speaker...*
What does the speaker mean by this? Be sure not to confuse the speaker with the author.

*The speaker is referring to...*
The answer will involve an outside text or cultural reference (an allusion).

*What does this word mean in context?*
Annotate for "million-dollar" words or unfamiliar terms—that way you will be more likely to recognize the context for the word right away. Make sure you're not just defining the word from memory. You must return to the passage and review the line in which the word appears, in addition to the lines above and below. Don't make assumptions about word meanings before returning to the passage to check.

*Dominant device*
Out of ALL of the answers below, what's the main literary device being used here? Note that there may be more than one device that is possible, but the answer here is the one that is the most important to the passage.

*Effect*

What is the lasting result of these lines on the passage?

*Infer* or *suggest*

What can we gather is true? Remember, when you make an inference, you are looking at information that is present in the passage to support an idea that the author doesn't directly state. This type of question requires more synthesis and analysis.

*Not* or *except*

These can be tricky. Eliminate all answers that are TRUE.

*The passage as a whole...*

The answer applies to the entire passage, not just one small part.

*Rhetorical function*

What's the purpose of this sentence, paragraph, or device? What does it do?

*Style*

Again, the answer must apply to the entire passage, not just part of it.

*Tone*

Be sure that you are responding correctly—does the test ask about the author's tone or the speaker's tone? Is it asking about the entire passage, a shift in tone, or a specific part of the passage.

If you learn to recognize these common phrases, you will be able to move much more quickly and confidently through the multiple choice section of the exam. Circle or underline these phrases when you see them, and look for the corresponding pieces in the answer choices.

# Examples of Common Question Stems

In order to make your life easier, and in order to help you do your very best on the test, it pays to understand the question stems, or the way that each question presents the problem. Each of these stems should

indicate they type of answer choice you are looking for. Here are some stems that you'll notice on the AP Exam:

The poem is best described as a...

The structure of the poem is determined by the speaker's...

The word [*word* (line numbers)] provides an example of...

The author's choice of words in the first paragraph can best be described as...

In a connotative sense, the adjective [*adjective* (line numbers)] refers to...

The shift in diction between the first paragraph and the final paragraph can best be described as...

In [line numbers] the tone can best be described as...

With the words [*poetic phrase here* (line numbers)], the speaker's attitude shifts from...

The tone of the passage as a whole shifts from...

The reader can infer that the character is concerned about [concern] by the way she...

It may be inferred from the first paragraph that the character will...

The words [*line from the passage* (line numbers)] imply that...

It may be inferred from the passage beginning with [*beginning lines* (line numbers)] that...

The description of the [*noun* (line numbers)] most directly suggests that it...

The word (*word* (line numbers)) refers to a...

In the content of the poem, the term [*word* (line numbers)] suggests...

The words [*words or phrases here* (line numbers)] serve to show...

The author's purpose in using a [literary device (line numbers)] is to...

When the syntax changes from short to longer sentences, this dichotomy in sentence structure best serves to...

The purpose of the character's action (line numbers) is to...

The character does this mainly to...

The author's main purpose in the first paragraph is to...

The primary purpose of the passage is to...

The function of the lines [*example from passage* (line numbers)] is to show that...

The function of the long sentence in (line numbers) is to reveal the character's...

The words [*words and phrases* (line numbers)] serve to...

The words [*words or phrase* (line numbers)] are an example of a...

The word [*word* (line numbers)] refers to the...

The first paragraph of the passage is mainly characterized by...

The words [*phrase* (line numbers)] contain examples of...

The literary device [*example of literary device from passage* (line numbers)] serves to...

The point of view of the passage is...

The narrator's perspective in the passage as a whole is that of...

The point of view in the passage as a whole shifts from...

# How to Answer Multiple-Choice Questions

When it comes to answering multiple-choice questions, there are a few useful tips you might want to keep in mind in order to achieve the highest grade possible:

**Pay attention to question structure.** In addition to there being only correct answer, there is always one wrong answer, one almost-right answer, and one opposite answer. If you immediately strike out answers that you know for sure are incorrect, you can usually eliminate two or three answer choices. If the option is completely foreign to you, it's probably a wrong answer.

**Be careful with absolutes.** Words like *always*, *never* or qualifiers like *often* frequently make a part of the answer wrong. Remember that if any portion of the answer is false, the whole answer is incorrect.

**Use the test to take the test.** Use information from other questions that you know the right answers to in order to answer questions that have you stumped.

**Look for similar answer questions.** If two choices closely resemble each other, one of them is usually the correct answer... or they are both completely wrong. That may sound unhelpful, but actually, if you notice that two choices look the same, it will help you also notice exactly what the differences between these choices are. Figure out which one answers the entirety of the question or which one is detailed enough to answer the precision of the question, or check to see if one or both are completely wrong.

**Pay attention to specific parts of the passage.** Check the first and last lines to determine how the writer introduced and closed the main concern of the piece.

**Make predictions.** If you know what sort of answer to expect, it is easier to eliminate wrong choices. Play "positive and negative" and eliminate the choices accordingly. For instance, if the speaker's tone is negative, eliminate all positive tone words like "satisfied." You can use this strategy with other opposites, too, like "long and short" (answers that are too short to fit the device o idea or answers that are too long when all that is needed is a word or two) or "too broad and too narrow" (choices that are either too general to answer the question or too specific and not targeting the question's stem); likewise, eliminate options that aren't mentioned at all.

**Look for outliers.** Completely wrong answers are usually irrelevant to the question at hand (or the passage itself), contradictory, or never addressed. Every question will have at least one answer choice that is completely wrong.

# Process of Elimination

POE means two things when it comes to the AP Lit test: Edgar Allen and Process of Elimination. In this portion of the review, we'll cover Process of Elimination. POE is your best friend when it comes to guessing aggressively and trying to obtain the maximum amount of points on the multiple choice section. If you can't locate the right answer right away, that's okay. Use your POE. Here's how you'd do it:

1. Read over each possible answer carefully.
2. Ask yourself what is wrong with the answer.
3. When you come across ideas that are inconsistent with the test, contain falsehoods, or seem to answer the opposite of the question, cross them out and eliminate them.
4. If you're left with one answer you're not 100% sure about, but you know that the others are all wrong, go with the one that you're not sure about. It sounds crazy, but it works because you know the others are wrong.
5. If you're left with more than one answer you're not positive about, you pick one. Yes, there's still a chance you'll get the answer wrong, but you simply don't have the time to investigate this response and making your best educated guess is better than leaving the bubble blank.

# Multiple-Choice Tips

**Get physical.** Always physically cross out answers that you know are incorrect. The act of crossing them out not only builds confidence towards finding the correct answer, it also helps you visually focus on the remaining choices.

Don't just cross out wrong answers. Circle or check right answers! Circle the part of the question that makes it correct and you will feel more confident and be more likely to get it right.

**Guess, no matter what.** Your grade will not be adversely affected for incorrect answers! You are only awarded points for questions that you answer correctly, which means it is to your absolute and total advantage to guess. You have a one-in-five chance of picking the right answer when you guess; you have a zero-in-five chance of picking the right answer when you skip over a question.

**Check your alignment.** There is nothing worse than getting to part of your test and seeing that you're on number seventeen on your answer key on number nineteen on your test. Before bubbling in your answer, make sure your answer sheet number corresponds with the number of the question you're answering.

**Pace yourself.** Answer one question per minute—remember, you can always guess, and you don't get penalized for incorrect answers. You do, however, earn your own penalty by leaving answers blank or by going so slowly that you neglect to get to the questions you can actually answer.

**Don't get stuck.** If you find yourself stuck on a particular question. Choose the best possible answer you can and, if you think you'll have time remaining, lightly circle the question number on your bubble sheet so you can easily go back and double-check your answer later.

**Don't freak out over long passages.** Just because a passage looks lengthy or difficult doesn't mean the questions are going to be more difficult.

**Don't read ahead.** Don't read the questions before you read the passage—time constraints do not allow for this and you may miss major

points of the passage by hunting-and-pecking…except in one certain instance (more on that shortly).

**Mark it up.** Go ahead and mark up the exam booklet—students who interact with the test generally perform better than those who do not.

# The Final Six Minutes

The one instance when it is ok to *hunt-and-peck* and jump straight to the questions is when you've got nothing left to lose: the last six minutes of the multiple-choice section.

The truth is that it may take an entire four or five minutes to read through and fully comprehend a passage—maybe you'll get to the first question or two, but by the time you're at question number four you'll hear *pencils down*. If you've only got six minutes left and you have passages left to read, try this strategy instead:

1. Skip the passage and scan the questions.
2. Determine which questions can be answered without doing a proper reading of the passage. Usually these are questions that ask for connotation, words in context, or identification of literary devices and their usage. Cross out the questions about theme, author's purpose, and the like.
3. Utilize the given line number and go straight to it to determine the connotation of a word or a word in context or definition, or to identify how an author is using a specific literary device.
4. Use the last few seconds of the test to bubble in the same answer for any answered questions you've got left—there's no guess penalty on AP Exams, so you can only help your score.

# Study Tool: Writing Practice Questions

One way to make sure you fully understand what the question is asking is to practice writing the questions yourself. After all, we learn best when we teach. By teaching yourself to write test questions, you'll be able to instantly decode whatever is being asked of you in the multiple-choice section. You can do this on an index card (to create flashcards for solo study) or you can just do it on paper.

For practice, choose a favorite poem or passage, then use the stems from the previous section to write questions. Next, write 5 possible answers (one correct and four incorrect). Try to write incorrect answers that might seem reasonable to a test-taker—you can think about aspects of the text you found particularly confusing or common errors you yourself have made on tests. The process of willfully misinterpreting the text can be just as useful as trying to interpret it correctly.

# five

# POETRY

It's safe to estimate that half of the literature on the AP exam comes from poetry: at least two poetry passages are included in the multiple-choice section and there's a poetry analysis question in the essay section. Generally, poems will come from the following areas (although there is some overlap):

- sixteenth century (think Edmund Spenser and Christopher Marlowe)
- seventeenth century (think Milton, Donne, Shakespeare)
- eighteenth century (think Blake, Keats, Wordsworth, Byron, Shelley, Coleridge)
- nineteenth century (think Emerson, Thoreau, Poe, Whitman, Emily Dickinson, Barrett
- twentieth century (think Maya Angelou, Billy Collins, Rita Dove, Edna St. Vincent Millay, Mary Oliver)
- female and minority writers (at least one selection, typically)
- religious texts (must be accessible to all students and questions will relate strictly to literary devices, meaning, and merit, not theology or doctrine)

According to the College Board, the following list of poets is a good starting place, in addition to the poets named above:

- W. H. Auden
- Elizabeth Bishop
- Anne Bradstreet
- Gwendolyn Brooks
- Robert Browning
- Lorna Dee Cervantes
- Geoffrey Chaucer
- Lucille Clifton
- H. D. (Hilda Doolittle)
- Paul Laurence Dunbar
- T. S. Eliot
- Robert Frost
- Joy Harjo
- Seamus Heaney
- George Herbert
- Garrett Hongo

- Gerard Manley Hopkins
- Langston Hughes
- Ben Jonson
- Philip Larkin
- Robert Lowell
- Andrew Marvell
- Marianne Moore
- Sylvia Plath
- Alexander Pope
- Adrienne Rich
- Anne Sexton
- Leslie Marmon Silko
- Cathy Song
- Wallace Stevens
- Alfred, Lord Tennyson
- Derek Walcott
- Walt Whitman
- Richard Wilbur
- William Carlos Williams
- William Butler Yeats

# Analyzing Poetry

Once you feel like you have a firm grasp on your literary terminology, you can begin to review poetry analysis strategies. These strategies will come in handy on all sections of your test, but TPCASTT might lend itself better to the poetry analysis essay merely because of the time constraints (and numerous passages) of the multiple-choice section. Since the entire test is checking to see if you can interpret poetry and draw conclusions, use the following suggestions.

## TPCASTT

This mnemonic device stands for:

- Title (what does it mean when it stands alone?)
- Paraphrase (translate each line of the poem into your own words)
- Connotation (how literary devices work to create meaning within the poem)
- Attitude (also known as tone)
- Shifts (how changes in things like structure, language, point of view, etc. effect the poem)
- Title re-evaluation
- Theme

How can you use TPCASTT on the AP Lit test? Begin by reading the poem to yourself, marking unfamiliar words or elements that just jump out at you. Then apply TPCASTT, beginning with the title. You won't have time to write paraphrases of each line, naturally, but you can just mentally translate as you go. By noting connotation, elements that contribute to tone, shifts, and theme along the way, you will have reviewed the poem substantially to draft a thoughtful essay.

## SOAPSTONE

There are usually multiple questions addressing the idea of tone on the AP Literature exam. Because tone usually comes from a combination of other, more concrete elements of a text, it helps to analyze those aspects with tone in mind. There are two different, quick-to-use techniques you can use immediately to complete a quick analysis and determine tone:

By putting the SOAPSTONE together, you can work quickly to analyze a text:

- Speaker
- Occasion
- Audience
- Purpose
- Subject
- TONE

SOAPSTONE works to help discover tone because it sets the piece in context, an important aspect of discovering tone.

## DIDLS

If finding the tone of a poem is still a problem area for you, try applying the DIDLS technique. DIDLS is another mnemonic device that you can remember quickly—and this trick can help you evaluate tone quickly on all portions of the exam.

The elements that establish tone are:

- Diction: How the author uses word choice to make his or her point. Diction can include the mood, attitude, dialect, and style of the writer's words.
- Imagery: Descriptive language that represents objects, actions and ideas by appealing directly to physical senses.
- Details: How particular items of information support the author's ideas or contribute to your overall impression of the text.
- Language: How the author uses language to convey his argument or ideas; for example, an author may use figurative language through similes and metaphors to make his writing more effective and persuasive.
- Syntax: The specific structure, order, and type of sentences in a text that spring from the rules of a language; the way that different parts of speech are put together in order to convey a complete thought.

For each of these, think about how the author uses the tools to convey his attitude about a specific topic.

Since you'll already be annotating for these elements, you can quickly think DIDLS and add the mnemonic together to see how the pieces work together to establish tone.

# How to Read a Poem
# (for the AP Test)

Poetry can be overwhelming, which is why you want to have a plan of attack ready on test day.

1. Always read the poem before you answer the questions.

2. Always read the poem two or three times if you are struggling with it or think you have the time.

3. Read the poem like it's a piece of prose and don't let form or structure get the best of you. (For example, you notice that it's a sonnet, and you know that you just hate sonnets, never understand the language, hate finding the turn or the meaning in the couplets—forget about all of that. View the piece as if it's a paragraph that somebody sliced into fourteen even strips and go from there).

4. When you read the poem the first time, don't annotate heavily. Read for basic understanding and obtain a sense of what's happening in the poem.

5. When you read the poem the second time, begin better annotations—just keep them quick. Go line-by-line, phrases by phrase. At this point, your biggest concern should be identifying the main idea of the poem and the tone of the poem, since you're guaranteed questions on those items.

6. If you have the opportunity to read a third time (or if you did not understand it from the first two reads), try to repeat Step 4 (line by line, phrase by phrase) quickly, without annotating. You don't have the privilege of going over a few lines that keep tripping you up, so this third review simply must be a quick one. Ignore those difficult lines and pay attention to the remainder of the poem. The idea here is that while there may certainly be questions about those lines you find challenging, the questions will not focus solely on those lines—there are going to be at least ten other questions about ten other aspects of the poem. If you do run into questions about the hard part, put your POE skills to use and move along.

> To read a poem as if it is prose, figure out where the sentences are and read punctuation mark-to-punctuation mark instead of line-to-line.

# Other Poetry Questions
# to Consider

**What are the main literary devices used in the passage?** You may want to note these while reading through the poem, which will benefit you when it comes time to address the actual questions.

**What is the central metaphor of the poem?** Sometimes poems are symbols of something greater, something outside of themselves. If you are able to determine the central metaphor of the piece, you will be able to answer a multitude of questions related to theme, tone, and purpose.

**What should I look for when it comes to the title?** Titles are important (unless you're talking about Emily Dickinson's work or Shakespeare's sonnets). An author assigns a title for a reason—if you can decipher the reason, you will once again gain insight into the metaphor, theme, tone, and purpose of the piece.

**What patterns or repeated elements occur in the poem?** Patterns and repetition found in poetry are not accidental: they serve a purpose. Perhaps the poet is trying to achieve a certain sound, or stress a point, or draw your focus to a message. Play detective and investigate the purpose of the repetition, because if it's there, you can be sure there will be questions about it to follow.

# Poetry Tips

Some people absolutely adore poetry; others find it to be a foreign language they'd like to avoid. Unfortunately for the latter, you won't find an AP Lit exam without poetry dotting the landscape at every page turn. However, you can make it easier on yourself by keeping the following tips in mind:

**Underline any foreign word.** If it's included in the poem, it's there for a reason (a reason you'll probably be tested on).

**Underline any unfamiliar word.** Likewise, if any word pops out at you simply because you don't remember what it means or because you've never seen it before, make a note of it in case you are asked to explain its definition in context.

**Know the structural differences between sonnet styles.** Make sure you read and review those Shakespearean and Petrarchan sonnets. More often than not, a sonnet will show up on the exam and you'll find a solid twelve to fifteen possible questions just about that one poem. You can't afford to skip out on fifteen total questions, so make sure you know and understand the differences.

**Look at the line breaks.** Poets end their lines at certain places for certain reasons: they're creating a rhyme scheme, or they're building a quick pace, or they're developing another sense of rhythm (the list goes on). If the line breaks seem quick, short, frequent, or something different altogether, they probably add to the meaning of the poem, which means you'll be asked about them.

**Paraphrase stanzas.** If a poem is comprised of several stanzas, make a general remark about the contents of the stanza (in your own words) and jot it down in the margin—this will not only help you recall the poem quickly, it will also help you build fluency and comprehension with the entirety of the piece.

# Poetry Strategies

On the AP Lit exam, you will be asked to read a poem or passage and then answer multiple-choice questions about it. There are several strategies you can use for this portion of the exam, which are listed below:

1. Read the first and last lines.
2. Pay attention to the poet's use of punctuation.
3. Read around the line number indicated in the question.
4. Use POE with positive and negatives.
5. Use POE with too broad and too narrow.
6. Ask *why would the author write this?*
7. Where are the shifts in subject or tone?
8. Find unusual words.
9. Look for extremes in answers.
10. Is the whole answer true?
11. Rephrase, restate, and say it all over it again.
12. What's the core literary device in this passage?
13. Are there any ironies in this poem?
14. Look at the title.
15. Look for patterns and repetition.

 EXAMPLE

For the following exercise, you will read a poem or a passage. You will not only need to address the AP-style question, but you will also need to decide which one of the multiple-choice strategies you should use to answer the question.

"I Wandered Lonely as a Cloud"
By William Wordsworth

*I wandered lonely as a cloud*
*That floats on high o'er vales and hills,*
*When all at once I saw a crowd,*
*A host, of golden daffodils;*
*Beside the lake, beneath the trees,*
*Fluttering and dancing in the breeze.*

Continuous as the stars that shine
And twinkle on the milky way,
They stretched in never-ending line
Along the margin of a bay:
Ten thousand saw I at a glance,
Tossing their heads in sprightly dance.

The waves beside them danced; but they
Out-did the sparkling waves in glee:
A poet could not but be gay,
In such a jocund company:
I gazed—and gazed—but little thought
What wealth the show to me had brought:

For oft, when on my couch I lie
In vacant or in pensive mood,
They flash upon that inward eye
Which is the bliss of solitude;
And then my heart with pleasure fills,
And dances with the daffodils.

1. The speaker's tone as he recounts the experiences with the daffodils in the poem is one of:

   A. childlike innocence

   B. careless indifference

   C. nostalgic reverence

   D. gently-controlled pity

   E. faintly satiric humor

   Strategy Used: _____ Answer _____

2. Which of the following illustrates the poetic device of personification?

   A. *heart with pleasure fills*

   B. *stretched in never-ending line*

   C. *tossing their heads in sprightly dance*

   D. *they flash upon that inward eye*

   E. *continuous as the stars that shine*

   Strategy Used: _____ Answer _____

GO ON

3. Which of the following is the best rendering of the phrase *I gazed—and gazed—but little thought/What wealth the show to me had brought?"*

A. The speaker paid little attention to what I was seeing.

B. At the time, the speaker didn't realize how valuable this moment was.

C. The speaker didn't think about how this would impact him later.

D. No matter how much he looked, the speaker didn't see anything special at the time.

E. We don't appreciate what we have.

Strategy Used: _____Answer_____

4. In context, the word *vacant* is best interpreted to mean:

A. empty

B. absent-minded

C. thoughtless

D. free

E. idle

Strategy Used: _____Answer_____

5. The speaker's experience as described in the final stanza is best characterized as:

A. a daydream induced by a long period of inactivity

B. an artistic experience resulting from the power of solitude

C. a heightened consciousness of the beauty of nature

D. a delusion brought about by deliriousness

E. a call to overcome his loneliness

Strategy Used: _____Answer_____

# six

# SHAKESPEARE AND DRAMA

**B**elieve it or not, plays count as prose on your AP exam. It is not unusual to find a passage from a play on the multiple-choice section or even the writing section. In addition to knowing your Shakespeare selections inside and out, here is a recommended list of playwrights and writers with whom you might want to become familiar:

- Aeschylus
- Edward Albee
- Amiri Baraka
- Samuel Beckett
- Anton Chekhov
- William Congreve
- Athol Fugard
- Lorraine Hansberry
- Lillian Hellman
- David Henry Hwang
- Henrik Ibsen
- Ben Jonson
- David Mamet
- Arthur Miller
- Molière

- Marsha Norman
- Sean O'Casey
- Eugene O'Neill
- Suzan-Lori Parks
- Harold Pinter
- Luigi Pirandello
- William Shakespeare
- George Bernard Shaw
- Sam Shepard
- Sophocles
- Tom Stoppard
- Luis Valdez
- Oscar Wilde
- Tennessee Williams
- August Wilson

## Common Plays

*King Lear* has appeared more frequently than any other Shakespearean play on the AP Lit exam, making a whopping fifteen occurrences since 1970. If you haven't read *King Lear* in class, then you should make time to read, study, and take notes on this play in your own time since there's a great chance you'll find it on the test. Coming in a strong second in appearances on the AP English Literature exam is none other than *Othello*. It's probable you've read *Othello* in class, but among Shakespeare's tragedies, this has the shortest cast, which means fewer characters to remember and more time for you to consider themes. *The Tempest* is the third most common Shakespearean play for AP Lit test-takers to run into, with six appearances, followed by *Hamlet* and *The Merchant of Venice*.

Since Arthur Miller, Tennessee Williams, and Henrik Ibsen all have plays that appeared five or more times on the test, these are not just "runner-ups" to Shakespeare—they are definitely important writers worth knowing and card reporting.

# seven

# STUDY STRATEGIES AND BEATING TEST ANXIETY

## Nine Ways To Beat Test Anxiety

Most of us suffer from some form of anxiety at one time or another. If you're enrolled in AP English Literature, chances are you're also enrolled in another AP class—you may even have a full AP load. With all the tests you have to take this year, the best thing you can do (aside from studying, that is) is to beat the test anxiety once and for all. Here's how.

1.  **Don't study the night before.** It might seem counter-intuitive, but all you will gain is more stress and less rest. If you're sleepy, tired, or overtired, you won't perform well on the test—how can you do your best when you're too tired to even be awake? Prepare ahead of time instead. The sooner you prepare for the exam, the more confident you'll become, and confidence is the best anxiety-buster.

2.  **Eat a protein-rich and complex-carb breakfast.** Feed your brain something other than facts and strategies to get going. Avoid sugar and caffeine to avoid crashing mid-exam. This may seem counter-intuitive—after all, coffee is what keeps you awake, right?—but, actually, sugar and caffeine are only quick fixes, and they will leave you with nothing left in the tank when they run out. Definitely avoid caffeine if you don't already regularly use it—it won't just make you jittery, but it's also a diuretic so it will make you have to use the bathroom, costing you valuable time.

3.  **Be comfortable.** Of all the days when you want to dress to impress a certain someone in class, today is not that day— put your focus on the task at hand and wear clothing that you can feel relaxed in.

4. **Go through your normal morning routine** (minus the caffeine, if you can go without it). Leave your house on time so that you don't feel rushed and worried about missing the test.

5. **Harness the power of positive thinking.** Plan to do well. Tell yourself you're going to do well. Keep telling yourself that until you believe it. Remember to repeat the following to yourself: *I know the structure of the exam, so there aren't going to be any surprises. I've been preparing for the exam, and students who prepare well score higher. A guess is better than an empty bubble.*

6. **Journal, journal, journal!** Recent research shows that students who spent ten to fifteen minutes before taking a test writing about their concerns and feelings relieved them of test anxiety. The science basically shows that their brainpower was liberated so that they could put it to use on the test (instead of letting anxiety occupy that space).

7. **Focus on YOU.** So someone else is writing furiously fast or already has their pencil down—so what? The AP test is not a measurement of how fast you go—it's about what and how you've learned. Take as much time as you're given and forget about everyone else. It's ok to be selfish right now.

8. **Let it be.** If you are a senior, by the time you take your AP test, you've likely been accepted to college and you probably know where you're going in the fall. The results of this test are not going to make or break your college career by a long shot, so take it easy. Avoid thinking things like *everything is riding on this.* That's simply not true. What's riding on it is maybe a few college credits. The reason this is a maybe has nothing to do with your score (well, maybe a little) and everything to do with the fact that some colleges have stringent policies about accepting AP credits—or they will still require you to take their own version of a particular courses. If you've taken AP Lit and demonstrated strong grades throughout the year, that's more important in the long run than the one test.

9. **Be sure to breathe.** When people get nervous, they tend to hold their breath, which increases stress, raises blood pressure, and can even cause a blackout. Please remember to breathe!

# A Step Above

Let's pretend that you're doing well on all of your practice exams in your AP class—and for this conversation, we'll say you're making a four (and yes, to all of you over-achievers or perfectionists out there, four is a fantastic score). Still, you're not quite satisfied and whatever the reason—self-motivation, perfectionism, parental pressure, college pressure, competition with your English nemesis—you want to get that five. Here are a few ways you can push that four over the edge to the top tier:

**Read the course description.** The course description (the one on the College Board website) not only details what the Board expects you to grasp firmly by the end of the course; it also contains additional AP-released tests, and the sooner you familiarize yourself with the test, the better (and the less anxious you will be). Reducing anxiety will help you perform better than usual on the test.

**Know your literary criticism.** If you know the difference between your New Critics and your New Historicists, and you can speak at length about the Feminists or the Psychoanalysts, see if you can include this knowledge in your essay. Most high school students—even AP students—don't name-drop literary movements in their essays, but if you can do it, go for it. Your reader will be impressed and will most likely reward you for it if you can do it well. But beware— don't name-drop for the sake of it; only do it if you can formulate some sort of intelligent conversation around it. Trying to use references to movements you don't understand can derail your argument and make you sound less knowledgeable than you actually are.

**Be sophisticated.** The College Board, along with the AP readers, love when students can show off a sophisticated writing style, which consists of elevated vocabulary (the million-dollar words used correctly) and varying sentence structures throughout the essays. Practice a few special sentence structures so you can bring them out easily for your essay. Even better if you can use techniques that partially mirror the style used by the author—this is a sophisticated way to show that you understand how an author develops and uses a style, and it shows off your own abilities. Additionally, if you can defend your thesis and organize your paper in a way that makes sense and steps away from the traditional five-paragraph form, all the better.

# PART II: TEST YOUR KNOWLEDGE

# eight

# PRACTICE TEST ONE

## Section I: One Hour

This section includes selections from literary works, followed by questions about their form, content, and style. After reading each selection, choose the best answer to each question.

Questions 1–15. Read the following poem carefully before choosing your answers.

**"To his Coy Mistress"**
By Andrew Marvell

(1) Had we but world enough, and time,
This coyness, lady, were no crime.
We would sit down and think which way
To walk, and pass our long love's day;
Thou by the Indian Ganges' side
Shouldst rubies find; I by the tide

(7) Of Humber would complain. I would
Love you ten years before the Flood;
And you should, if you please, refuse
Till the conversion of the Jews.
My vegetable love should grow
Vaster than empires, and more slow

(13) An hundred years should go to praise
Thine eyes, and on thy forehead gaze;
Two hundred to adore each breast,
But thirty thousand to the rest;
An age at least to every part,
And the last age should show your heart.

(19) For, lady, you deserve this state,
Nor would I love at lower rate.

(21) But at my back I always hear
Time's winged chariot hurrying near;
And yonder all before us lie
Deserts of vast eternity.

(25) Thy beauty shall no more be found,
Nor, in thy marble vault, shall sound
My echoing song; then worms shall try
That long preserv'd virginity,
And your quaint honour turn to dust,
And into ashes all my lust.

(31) The grave's a fine and private place,
But none I think do there embrace.
Now therefore, while the youthful hue
Sits on thy skin like morning dew,
And while thy willing soul transpires
At every pore with instant fires,

(37) Now let us sport us while we may;
And now, like amorous birds of prey,
Rather at once our time devour,
Than languish in his slow-chapp'd power.
Let us roll all our strength, and all
Our sweetness, up into one ball;

(43) And tear our pleasures with rough strife
Thorough the iron gates of life.
Thus, though we cannot make our sun
Stand still, yet we will make him run.

1.  In lines 20–30 the tone of the passage shifts from
    _____ to _____.

    (A) admiration to admonition
    (B) praising to disbelieving
    (C) loving to cautious
    (D) ingratiating to indifferent
    (E) enamored to disgusted

2.  In line 29, *quaint honor* symbolizes

    (A) virtue
    (B) life
    (C) virginity
    (D) youth
    (E) respect

3.  The primary metaphor in the first twelve lines is:

    (A) the Flood
    (B) the Ganges
    (C) Humber
    (D) conversion
    (E) vegetable love

4.  What is the intended effect of the contrast in
    lines 5–10?

    (A) to demonstrate the intensity of his
        emotional plea
    (B) to illustrate a sense of urgency
    (C) to convey patience in contrary
        circumstances
    (D) to amplify the coyness of the mistress
    (E) to serve as a foil

5.  The author creates a sense of urgency through
    an allusion to Greek mythology when he says:

    (A) *by the Indian Ganges* (line 5)
    (B) *the tide of Humber* (lines 6-7)
    (C) *the last age* (line 18)
    (D) *Time's winged chariot hurrying near* (line 22)
    (E) *deserts of vast eternity* (line 24)

6.  Which of the following statements best reflects
    the speaker's attitude?

    (A) Honor and virtue are worthy of
        preservation.
    (B) Love frequently presents challenges of
        endurance.
    (C) Patience is a virtue best forgotten in love.
    (D) Time knows no bounds in love.
    (E) Time requires us to accept when the
        opportunity for love arises.

7.  What is the dominant literary device used in
    lines 1-10?

    (A) imagery
    (B) rhyme scheme
    (C) iambic pentameter
    (D) hyperbole
    (E) metaphor

8.  Which of the following lines contain internal
    rhyme?

    (A) *This coyness, lady, were no crime* (line 2).
    (B) *To walk, and pass our long love's day* (line 4)
    (C) *Shouldst rubies find; I by the tide* (line 6)
    (D) *and you should, if you please, refuse* (line 9)
    (E) *but thirty thousand to the rest* (line 16).

9. The purpose of the allusions in lines 5-8 is to:

(A) persuade

(B) compliment

(C) shock

(D) elevate

(E) respect

10. In the last lines of the passage, the author invigorates the speaker's message by employing all of the following, except:

(A) pun

(B) simile

(C) alliteration

(D) end rhyme

(E) allegory

11. The style of this poem most closely resembles a(n):

(A) sonnet

(B) lyric poem

(C) elegy

(D) ode

(E) ballad

12. The simile in line 34 reveals that the speaker is:

(A) ambitious

(B) discontented

(C) inspirited

(D) sophisticated

(E) puerile

13. The phrase *till the conversion of the Jews* is an example of:

(A) understatement

(B) hyperbole

(C) symbolism

(D) internal characterization

(E) metaphor

14. In the title, the word *coy* most likely means:

(A) modest

(B) virtuous

(C) shy

(D) seductive

(E) hesitant

15. The author wrote the poem using:

(A) iambic pentameter

(B) iambic tetrameter.

(C) anapestic trimeter

(D) dactylic dimeter

(E) trochaic monometer

GO ON

Questions 16–29. Read the following poem carefully before choosing your answers.

## "Spring and All"
### By William Carlos Williams

(1) By the road to the contagious hospital
under the surge of the blue
mottled clouds driven from the
northeast—a cold wind. Beyond, the
waste of broad, muddy fields
brown with dried weeds, standing and fallen

(7) patches of standing water
the scattering of tall trees

(9) All along the road the reddish
purplish, forked, upstanding, twiggy
stuff of bushes and small trees
with dead, brown leaves under them
leafless vines—

(14) Lifeless in appearance, sluggish
dazed spring approaches—

(16) They enter the new world naked,
cold, uncertain of all
save that they enter. All about them
the cold, familiar wind—

(20) Now the grass, tomorrow
the stiff curl of wildcarrot leaf

(22) One by one objects are defined—
It quickens: clarity, outline of leaf

(24) But now the stark dignity of
entrance—Still, the profound change
has come upon them: rooted they
grip down and begin to awake.

16. It is likely that the *contagious hospital* (line 1) is a symbol for:

    (A) an epidemic
    (B) the effect of war
    (C) the modern world
    (D) popular philosophies
    (E) the government

17. What atmosphere or mood is created by the phrase *the surge of the blue mottled clouds*?

    (A) cogent and telling
    (B) domineering and stirring
    (C) ominous and foreboding
    (D) bleak and austere
    (E) anemic and monotonous

18. The diction in the first stanza (lines 1-7) indicates that the speaker:

    (A) suffers from a contagious ailment
    (B) has a sense of hopefulness
    (C) feels discouraged by the landscape
    (D) has difficulty seeing any order
    (E) feels overwhelmed by the idea of death

19. The overarching archetype of this poem could best be described as:

    (A) good prevails over evil
    (B) man's loss and eventual return
    (C) the ability to transform
    (D) rite of passage
    (E) liberating truth

20. The tone of the poem shifts from one of _____ to _____.

    (A) fatalism to rapture
    (B) lethargy to sagacity
    (C) tragedy to enlightenment
    (D) ponderousness to respectfulness
    (E) moroseness to admiration

21. What type of setting does the author describe in this poem?

    (A) desolate
    (B) apocalyptic
    (C) bleak
    (D) somber
    (E) haunting

22. The phrase *it quickens* (line 30) refers to:

    (A) the pace of the events

    (B) the revival of nature

    (C) the animation of the setting

    (D) the acuteness of the speaker's vision

    (E) the hastening of the speaker's emotions

23. The word *save* on line 23 means:

    (A) redeem

    (B) except

    (C) rescue

    (D) store

    (E) extricate

24. What does spring symbolize in this poem?

    (A) the onset of modern thinking

    (B) the immunization from the contagious disease

    (C) the revitalization of medicine

    (D) the consummation of the poetic experience

    (E) the outgrowth of verdant life

25. The image of the *stiff curl* indicates:

    (A) a furl

    (B) an unfolding

    (C) an elaboration

    (D) a stagnation

    (E) a withdrawal

26. Which of the following statements best represents the theme of the poem?

    (A) Observations are necessary for maturation.

    (B) Death ultimately leads to renewal.

    (C) Man must step out of human spaces to pay attention to the natural world.

    (D) Nature has a transformative effect on man.

    (E) Man never notices the passage of time without being in nature.

27. The lines *dazed spring* and *They enter the new world naked* (15 and 16) contain examples of:

    (A) symbolism

    (B) simile

    (C) personification

    (D) allegory

    (E) anaphora

28. The entirety of the poem could best be described as:

    (A) an allegory

    (B) a metaphor

    (C) a symbol

    (D) a satire

    (E) a conceit

29. Lines 17-20 seem to indicate that the speaker looks upon the scene with:

    (A) compassion

    (B) curiosity

    (C) certainty

    (D) surprise

    (E) fascination

GO ON

Questions 30-41. Read the following passage and think carefully before choosing your answers.

## Excerpt from *Madame Bovary*
### By Gustave Flaubert

(1) We were in class when the head-master came in, followed by a "new fellow," not wearing the school uniform, and a school servant carrying a large desk. Those who had been asleep woke up, and every one rose as if just surprised at his work. The head-master

(7) made a sign to us to sit down. Then, turning to the classmaster, he said to him in a low voice: "Monsieur Roger, here is a pupil whom I recommend to your care; he'll be in the second. If his work and conduct are satisfactory, he will go into one of the upper classes, as becomes his age."

(14) The "new fellow," standing in the corner behind the door so that he could hardly be seen, was a country lad of about fifteen, and taller than any of us. His hair was cut square on his forehead like a village chorister's; he looked reliable, but very ill at ease. Although he was not broad-shouldered,

(21) his short school jacket of green cloth with black buttons must have been tight about the armholes, and showed at the opening of the cuffs red wrists accustomed to being bare. His legs, in blue stockings, looked out from beneath yellow trousers, drawn tight by braces. He wore stout, ill-cleaned, hobnailed boots.

(29) We began repeating the lesson. He listened with all his ears, as attentive as if at a sermon, not daring even to cross his legs or lean on his elbow; and when at two o'clock the bell rang, the master was obliged to tell him to fall into line with the rest of us.

(35) When we came back to work, we were in the habit of throwing our caps on the floor so as to have our hands more free; we used from the door to toss them under the form, so that they hit against the wall and made a lot of dust: it was "the thing."

(41) But, whether he had not noticed the trick, or did not dare to attempt it, the "new fellow" was still holding his cap on his knees even after prayers were over. It was one of those head-gears of composite order, in which we can find traces of the bearskin, shako, billycock hat, sealskin cap, and

(48) cotton nightcap; one of those poor things, in fine, whose dumb ugliness has depths of expression, like an imbecile's face. Oval, stiffened with whalebone, it began with three round knobs; then came in succession lozenges of velvet and rabbit-skin separated by a red band; after that a sort of bag that

(55) ended in a cardboard polygon covered with complicated braiding, from which hung, at the end of a long, thin cord, small twisted gold threads in the manner of a tassel. The cap was new; its peak shone.

30. The passage is written from which point of view?

   (A) first-person
   (B) third-person omniscient
   (C) third-person limited
   (D) objective
   (E) first-person limited

31. The tone of the passage could best be described as:

   (A) attentive
   (B) critical
   (C) sentimental
   (D) detached
   (E) informal

32. The author uses all of the following devices except _____ to characterize the boy.

    (A) imagery

    (B) simile

    (C) appearance

    (D) contrast

    (E) dialogue

33. The last sentence, *The cap was new; its peak shone*, reveals that the speaker's attitude towards the boy is

    (A) amused

    (B) respectful

    (C) understanding

    (D) pious

    (E) esteemed

34. The description in lines 14-34 indicates that the new boy:

    (A) did not concern himself with social acceptance

    (B) feared his classmates

    (C) was a conscientious student

    (D) possessed honor

    (E) respected his surroundings

35. The speaker and the boy differ in all of the following ways except:

    (A) socio-economic background

    (B) academic performance

    (C) levels of respect

    (D) upbringing

    (E) appearance

36. The word *lozenges* in line 53 most likely means:

    (A) medicine

    (B) heraldry

    (C) windowpane

    (D) stone

    (E) diamond

37. The author utilizes all of the following except:

    (A) simile

    (B) imagery

    (C) dialogue

    (D) details

    (E) metaphor

38. Which literary technique does the author employ in lines 14-28?

    (A) simile

    (B) narrative

    (C) imagery

    (D) indirection characterization

    (E) figurative language

39. What can be inferred about the new fellow by the author's use of quotation marks around the phrase *new fellow*?

    (A) He is not well-received by his peers.

    (B) He is someone with whom the speaker is familiar.

    (C) His name is unknown to the speaker.

    (D) He is smaller and younger than the rest of the class.

    (E) He is one of many new students.

40. The purpose of the passage is to:

    (A) introduce the reader to a new character

    (B) convey the differences between the speaker and character

    (C) foreshadow interactions between the speaker and character

    (D) describe what used to be a common school day

    (E) indicate how new students were treated previously

41. The word *chorister* (line 18) most likely means:

    (A) singer

    (B) laborer

    (C) servant

    (D) messenger

    (E) entertainer

Questions 42-55. Read the following passage and think carefully before choosing your answers.

## Excerpt from *William Wilson*
### By Edgar Allen Poe

(1) Let me call myself, for the present, William Wilson. The fair page now lying before me need not be sullied with my real appellation. This has been already too much an object for the scorn, for the horror, for the detestation of my race. To the uttermost regions of the

(7) globe have not the indignant winds bruited its unparalleled infamy? Oh, outcast of all outcasts most abandoned! To the earth art thou not forever dead? to its honors, to its flowers, to its golden aspirations? and a cloud, dense, dismal, and limitless, does it not hang eternally between thy hopes and heaven?

(14) I would not, if I could, here or to-day, embody a record of my later years of unspeakable misery, and unpardonable crime. This epoch—these later years—took unto themselves a sudden elevation in turpitude, whose origin alone it is my present purpose to assign. Men usually grow base by degrees.

(21) From me, in an instant, all virtue dropped bodily as a mantle. I shrouded my nakedness in triple guilt. From comparatively trivial wickedness I passed, with the stride of a giant, into more than the enormities of an Elah-Gabalus. What chance—what one event brought this evil thing to pass, bear with me

(28) while I relate. Death approaches; and the shadow which foreruns him has thrown a softening influence over my spirit. I long, in passing through the dim valley, for the sympathy—I had nearly said for the pity—of my fellow-men. I would fain have them believe that I have been, in some measure, the

(35) slave of circumstances beyond human control. I would wish them to seek out for me, in the details I am about to give, some little oasis of fatality amid a wilderness of error. I would have them allow—what they cannot refrain from allowing—that, although temptation may have erewhile existed as great, man was

(42) never thus, at least, tempted before—certainly, never thus fell. And it is therefore that he has never thus suffered. Have I not indeed been living in a dream? And am I not now dying a victim to the horror and the mystery of the wildest of all sublunary visions?

(48) I am the descendant of a race whose imaginative and easily excitable temperament has at all times rendered them remarkable; and, in my earliest infancy, I gave evidence of having fully inherited the family character. As I advanced in years it was more strongly developed; becoming, for many reasons, a

(55) cause of serious disquietude to my friends, and of positive injury to myself. I grew self-willed, addicted to the wildest caprices, and a prey to the most ungovernable passions. Weak-minded, and beset with constitutional infirmities akin to my own, my parents could do but little to check the evil propensities which distinguished me. Some

(63) feeble and ill-directed efforts resulted in complete failure on their part, and, of course, in total triumph on mine. Thenceforward my voice was a household law; and at an age when few children have abandoned their leading-strings, I was left to the guidance of my own will, and became, in all but name, the master of my own actions.

(71) My earliest recollections of a school-life are connected with a large, rambling, cottage-built, and somewhat decayed building in a misty-looking village of England, where were a vast number of gigantic and gnarled trees, and where all the houses were excessively ancient. In truth, it was a dream-like and spirit-soothing place, that venerable old town. At this moment,

(80) in fancy, I feel the refreshing chilliness of its deeply-shadowed avenues, inhale the fragrance of its thousand shrubberies, and thrill anew with undefinable delight, at the deep, hollow note of the church-bell, breaking, each hour, with sullen and sudden roar, upon the stillness of the dusky atmosphere in which the old, fretted, Gothic steeple lay imbedded and asleep.

(89) It gives me, perhaps, as much of pleasure as I can now in any manner experience, to dwell upon minute recollections of the school and its concerns. Steeped in misery as I am—misery, alas! only too real—I shall be pardoned for seeking relief, however slight and temporary, in the weakness of a few (96) rambling details. These, moreover, utterly trivial, and even ridiculous in themselves, assume, to my fancy, adventitious importance as connected with a period and a locality, when and where I recognize the first ambiguous monitions of the destiny which afterwards so fully overshadowed me. Let me then remember.

(104) The house, I have said, was old, irregular, and cottage-built. The grounds were extensive, and an enormously high and solid brick wall, topped with a bed of mortar and broken glass, encompassed the whole. This prison-like rampart formed the limit of our domain. Beyond it we saw but thrice a

(111) week—once every Saturday afternoon, when, c paradox, too utterly monstrous for solution! attended by two ushers, we were permitted to take brief walks in a body through some of the neighbouring fields—and twice during Sunday, when we were paraded in the same formal manner to the morning and evening (118) service in the one church of the village. Of this church the principal of our school was pastor. With how deep a spirit of wonder and perplexity was I wont to regard him from our remote pew in the gallery, as, with step solemn and slow, he ascended the pulpit! This reverend man, with countenance so (125) demurely benign, with robes so glossy and so clerically flowing, with wig so minutely powdered, so rigid and so vast—could this be he who of late, with sour visage, and in snuffy habiliments, administered, ferule in hand, the Draconian laws of the academy? Oh, gigantic paradox, too utterly monstrous for solution!

42. Based on lines 53-62, we can infer that the speaker:

(A) enjoys his doppelganger

(B) questions his true identity

(C) seeks to protect his conscious self from the truth

(D) has been institutionalized

(E) committed crimes in the past

43. This passage is concerned with:

(A) the effects of education in the later years

(B) the conscience's psychological traps

(C) maintaining an alter ego

(D) finding solutions for paradoxical issues

(E) overcoming guilt

44. The primary metaphor for William Wilson in this passage is:

(A) a decayed building

(B) gnarled trees

(C) a venerable village

(D) a cottage-built house

(E) a remote pew

45. The genre of this story is most likely

(A) historical fiction

(B) romantic

(C) mystery

(D) horror

(E) Gothic fiction

GO ON

46. The attitude of the speaker can best be described as:

    (A) disinterested

    (B) crafty

    (C) cynical

    (D) self-aware

    (E) vengeful

47. The theme of the passage centers on:

    (A) the ambiguity between love and hate

    (B) the importance of emotions to the self

    (C) the inclination to reject hatred

    (D) the lasting effects of time's passage

    (D) the danger of self-denial

48. The word *constitutional* in line 60 means:

    (A) essential

    (B) organized

    (C) inherent

    (D) authorized

    (E) governing

49. The author uses indirect characterization to reveal _____:

    (A) acts about the speaker's childhood

    (B) the insanity of the speaker

    (C) how the speaker controls his own world

    (D) the speaker's affinity towards academia

    (E) the nostalgic fondness the speaker has towards his youth

50. The purpose of lines (43-50) is to:

    (A) reveal how close familial ties influence thought and behavior

    (B) speak to man's ability to ignore evidence in the name of wishful thinking

    (C) display the pride the speaker possesses regarding his lineage

    (D) explain that being overcome with emotion can result in greatness

    (E) allow the reader to convince himself that all will be well

51. The point of view in this story:

    (A) first-person limited

    (B) first-person omniscient

    (C) second person

    (D) third-person limited

    (E) third-person omniscient

52. In this passage, the wall functions as:

    (A) a comparison of reality and imaginary

    (B) an image of death and mortality

    (C) an emblem of educational institutions

    (D) a symbol of entrapment

    (E) a metaphor for the speaker

53. We understand that William Wilson is not the narrator's real name because of lines:

    (A) 17-20

    (B) 4-6

    (C) 1-2

    (D) 56-59

    (E) 104-105

54. The antecedent for the word *their* in line 64 is:

    (A) efforts

    (B) propensities

    (C) failure

    (D) parents

    (E) infirmities

55. The word *sublunary* in line 47 means:

    (A) terrestrial

    (B) fleeting

    (C) non-temporal

    (D) anthropic

    (E) utopian

# Section II: One Hour

This section includes selections from literary works, followed by questions that will ask you to address their form, content, and style. After reading each selection, craft a well-written essay that responds to the question.

Poetry: Though written by two different poets, the following poems function as companion poems. In a well-organized essay, distinguish between the attitudes expressed in the poems and discuss the techniques that the poets use to present these attitudes. Be sure to support your statements with specific references.

### "The Passionate Shepherd To His Nymph"
by Christopher Marlowe

(1) Come live with me and be my love,
And we will all the pleasures prove
That valleys, groves, hills, and fields
Woods or steepy mountain yields
And we will sit upon the rocks,
Seeing the shepherds feed their flocks

(7) By shallow rivers to whose falls
Melodious birds sing madrigals.
And I will make thee beds of roses
And a thousand fragrant posies,
A cap of flower, and a kirtle
Embroidered all with leaves of myrtle;

(13) A gown made of the finest wool
Which from our pretty lambs we pull;
Fair lined slippers for the cold
With buckles of the purest gold;
A belt of straw and ivy buds,
With coral clasps and amber studs;

(19) And if these pleasures may thee move,
Come live with me and be my love.
The shepherds' swains shall dance and sing
For thy delight each May morning:
If these delights thy mind may move,
Then live with me and be my love.

### "The Nymph's Reply to the Shepherd"
Sir Walter Raleigh

(1) If all the world and love were young,
And truth in every shepherd's tongue,
These pretty pleasures might me move
To live with thee and be thy love.
Time drives the flocks from field to fold,
When rivers rage and rocks grow cold;

(7) And Philomel becometh dumb;
The rest complain of cares to come.
The flowers do fade, and wanton fields
To wayward winter reckoning yields;
A honey tongue, a heart of gall,
Is fancy's spring, but sorrow's fall.

(13) Thy gowns, thy shoes, thy bed of roses,
Thy cap, thy kirtle, and thy posies,
Soon break, soon wither, soon forgotten,
In folly ripe, in reason rotten.
Thy belt of straw and ivy buds,
Thy coral clasps and amber studs,

(19) All these in me no means can move
To come to thee and be thy love.
But could youth last and love still breed,
Had joys no date nor age no need,
Then these delights my mind might move
To live with thee and be thy love.

GO ON

Prose: Read the following passage and write a well-organized essay in which you demonstrate how the author uses literary techniques to reveal the speaker's attitude towards her aunt.

## Except from *Jane Eyre*
Charlotte Brontë

(1) "I am not deceitful; if I were, I should say I loved you; but I declare I do not love you; I dislike you the worst of anybody in the world except John Reed; and this book about the liar, you may give it to your girl, Georgiana, for it is she who tells lies, and not... I am glad you are no relation of mine; I will never call

(8) you aunt again as long as I live; I will never come to see you when I am grown up; and if anyone asks me how I liked you, and how you treated me, I will say the very thought of you makes me sick, and that you treated me with miserable cruelty... How dare I, Mrs. Reed? How dare I? Because it is the truth. You think that I have no feelings, and that I

(16) can live without one bit of love or kindness; but I cannot live so; and you have no pity. I shall remember how you thrust me back— roughly and violently thrust me back into the red-room, and locked me up there—to my dying day; though I was in agony; though I cried out, while suffocating with distress, 'Have mercy! Have mercy, Aunt Reed!' And

(24) that punishment you made me suffer because your wicked boy struck me—knocked me down for nothing. I will tell anybody who asks me questions, this exact tale. People think you a good woman; but you are bad— hard-hearted. You are deceitful!"

Open Answer: Albert Einstein said, "Look deep into nature, and you will understand everything better." In literature, characters are prone to escape into the green world to understand "everything better." Choose a novel or a play in which a scene or character displays the escape into the green world in order to achieve a greater sense of understanding.

## Answer Key (Practice Test One)

| | | | | | | |
|---|---|---|---|---|---|---|
| 1. | (A) | 20. | (E) | 39. | (B) |
| 2. | (C) | 21. | (D) | 40. | (B) |
| 3. | (E) | 22. | (B) | 41. | (A) |
| 4. | (C) | 23. | (B) | 42. | (C) |
| 5. | (E) | 24. | (A) | 43. | (B) |
| 6. | (E) | 25. | (B) | 44. | (D) |
| 7. | (D) | 26. | (C) | 45. | (E) |
| 8. | (D) | 27. | (C) | 46. | (D) |
| 9. | (A) | 28. | (A) | 47. | (B) |
| 10. | (C) | 29. | (A) | 48. | (C) |
| 11. | (B) | 30. | (A) | 49. | (B) |
| 12. | (A) | 31. | (B) | 50. | (B) |
| 13. | (B) | 32. | (E) | 51. | (A) |
| 14. | (A) | 33. | (C) | 52. | (D) |
| 15. | (B) | 34. | (D) | 53. | (C) |
| 16. | (C) | 35. | (B) | 54. | (D) |
| 17. | (D) | 36. | (E) | 55. | (A) |
| 18. | (D) | 37. | (E) | | |
| 19. | (B) | 38. | (D) | | |

# nine

# PRACTICE TEST TWO

## Section I: One Hour

**This section includes selections from literary works, followed by questions about their form, content, and style. After reading each selection, choose the best answer to each question.**

Questions 1–13. Read the following poem carefully before choosing your answers.

### "After Apple-Picking"
### by Robert Frost

(1) My long two-pointed ladder's sticking
    through a tree
Toward heaven still.
And there's a barrel that I didn't fill
Beside it, and there may be two or three
Apples I didn't pick upon some bough.
But I am done with apple-picking now.

(7) Essence of winter sleep is on the night,
The scent of apples; I am drowsing off.
I cannot shake the shimmer from my sight
I got from looking through a pane of glass
I skimmed this morning from the
    water-trough,
And held against the world of hoary grass.
It melted, and I let it fall and break.

(14) But I was well
Upon my way to sleep before it fell,
And I could tell
What form my dreaming was about to take.
The woodchuck could say whether it's
    like his
Magnified apples appear and reappear,
Stem end and blossom end,

(21) And every fleck of russet showing clear.
My instep arch not only keeps the ache,
It keeps the pressure of a ladder-round.
And I keep hearing from the cellar-bin
That rumbling sound
Of load on load of apples coming in.
For I have had too much

(28) Of apple-picking; I am overtired
Of the great harvest I myself desired.
There were ten thousand thousand fruit to
    touch,
Cherish in hand, lift down, and not let fall,
For all
That struck the earth,
No matter if not bruised, or spiked with
    stubble,

(35) Went surely to the cider-apple heap
As of no worth.
One can see what will trouble
This sleep of mine, whatever sleep it is.
Were he not gone,
Long sleep, as I describe its coming on,
Or just some human sleep.

1. In lines 30-31, the speaker's attitude towards his work could best be described as:

(A) judicious and shrewd

(B) fond and attentive

(C) careful and precise

(D) keen and astute

(E) loving and nostalgic

2. The shift on line 13 signifies:

(A) that the dream experience is equal to the work experience

(B) the speaker's difficulty differentiating between imagination and reality

(C) how increased labor results can result in manic episodes

(D) how the speaker treasures his vocation

(E) that the speaker has a strong desire to pursue another vocation

3. The word *overtired* in line 28 indicates the speaker's sense of:

(A) sleepiness

(B) exhaustion

(C) satisfaction

(D) crankiness

(E) boredom

4. The last line of the poem suggests the speaker wonders if:

(A) Unanswered questions can be answered through rest.

(B) There is life after death.

(C) Sleep cures plaguing ailments.

(D) It is possible to achieve a hibernation-like state.

(E) He will die soon.

5. The intended effect of repetition in lines 38-41 is:

(A) fear

(B) anticipation

(C) exhaustion

(D) anxiety

(E) sadness

6. Which of the following lines contains hyperbole?

(A) line 1

(B) line 5

(C) line 15

(D) line 27

(E) line 34

7. The word *hoary* on line 13 most likely means:

(A) green

(B) decaying

(C) recent

(D) silver

(E) old

8. Which of the following devices enhances the speaker's point in the last two lines of the passage?

(A) personification

(B) repetition

(C) figure of speech

(D) irony

(E) assonance

9. The structure and rhyme scheme of the poem contribute to the poem's overall sense of:

(A) uncertainty

(B) chaos

(C) dreaming

(D) conflict

(E) sentimentality

10. The apples that have touched the ground symbolize:

   (A) the speaker's sin

   (B) original sin

   (C) the speaker's indifference

   (D) the speaker's dissatisfaction

   (E) the banality of evil

11. Based on lines 1–5, one may infer that the speaker:

   (A) knows the apple-picking season is ending

   (B) may retire from his duties as an apple-picker

   (C) has fulfilled all of his obligations to the season and to himself

   (D) realizes that his death is approaching

   (E) attaches sentimental value to his work

12. *My long two-pointed ladder's sticking through a tree/ Toward heaven still* reveals:

   (A) a suspension in time

   (B) suspension between reality and imagination

   (C) a sense of struggle

   (D) a sense of moral aspiration

   (E) the struggle to remain virtuous in labor

13. The most likely connotation of the word *winter* (line 7) is:

   (A) coolness

   (B) stillness

   (C) reflection

   (D) ending

   (E) death

Questions 14–25. Read the following poem carefully before choosing your answers.

### "A Woman's Shortcomings"
#### by Elizabeth Barrett Browning

(1)  She has laughed as softly as if she sighed,
     She has counted six, and over,
     Of a purse well filled, and a heart well tried—
     Oh, each a worthy lover!
     They "give her time"; for her soul must slip
     Where the world has set the grooving;
     She will lie to none with her fair red lip:
     But love seeks truer loving.

(9)  She trembles her fan in a sweetness dumb,
     As her thoughts were beyond recalling;
     With a glance for one, and a glance for some,
     From her eyelids rising and falling;
     Speaks common words with a blushful air,
     Hears bold words, unreproving;
     But her silence says—what she never will
       swear—
     And love seeks better loving.

(17) Go, lady! lean to the night-guitar,
     And drop a smile to the bringer;
     Then smile as sweetly, when he is far,
     At the voice of an in-door singer.

     Bask tenderly beneath tender eyes;
     Glance lightly, on their removing;
     And join new vows to old perjuries—
     But dare not call it loving!

(25) Unless you can think, when the song is done,
     No other is soft in the rhythm;
     Unless you can feel, when left by One,
     That all men else go with him;
     Unless you can know, when unpraised by his
       breath,
     That your beauty itself wants proving;
     Unless you can swear "For life, for death!"—
     Oh, fear to call it loving!

(33) Unless you can muse in a crowd all day
     On the absent face that fixed you;
     Unless you can love, as the angels may,
     With the breadth of heaven betwixt you;
     Unless you can dream that his faith is fast,
     Through behoving and unbehoving;
     Unless you can die when the dream is past—
     Oh, never call it loving!

14. *Six and over* in line 2 refers to:

    (A) musings

    (B) shortcomings

    (C) laughs

    (D) marriage proposals

    (E) suitors

15. The most likely meaning for *grooving* in line 6 is:

    (A) dance pattern

    (B) rhythm

    (C) channel

    (D) routine

    (E) pleasure

16. In lines 21-23, the speaker:

    (A) advises that flirtation leads to false feelings

    (B) cautions not to confuse infatuation with love

    (C) reveals her disdain for common courtship habits

    (D) admonishes those who partake in casual courting

    (E) honors the sanctity of marriage vows

17. The final stanza could best be summarized by which one of the following statements?

    (A) Do not fall victim to craftiness.

    (B) There is no such thing as true romantic love.

    (C) Love occurs outside of traditional expectations.

    (D) Real love takes places in another realm.

    (E) Life exists beyond the bounds of love.

18. One can infer that *new vows to old perjuries* (line 23) means:

    (A) One promising the same thing without change.

    (B) New love erases former mistakes.

    (C) Women quickly fall for mens' tricks.

    (D) Men fall quickly for womens' tricks.

    (E) Forgiveness is the key to finding love.

19. Which of the following is the main literary device employed by the author?

    (A) imagery

    (B) characterization

    (C) rhythm

    (D) rhyme scheme

    (E) incremental repetition

20. The second stanza contains all of the following devices except:

    (A) rhyme scheme

    (B) meter

    (C) repetition

    (D) trope

    (E) metaphor

21. The author indicates that a woman's shortcomings:

    (A) include a fear of being independent

    (B) involve hesitancy towards self-advocacy

    (C) develop from societal expectations

    (D) encourage a willingness to abandon ideals

    (E) begin with the self

22. The *absent face* in line 34 refers to:

    (A) one who looked upon the speaker absentmindedly

    (B) one who is not in visible sight

    (C) one who did not employ traditional wooing techniques

    (D) one who does not readily express emotion

    (E) one who chooses another

23. It can be inferred that the speaker is addressing:

    (A) an ingénue

    (B) women at large

    (C) an enemy

    (D) a hopeless romantic

    (E) her daughter

24. What statement does the speaker make about love?

(A) be cautious when choosing a spouse

(B) love is worthless unless is remains eternal

(C) following societal relationship rules is foolish

(D) women are responsible for their own heartaches

(E) real love is logically unattainable

25. The word *unreproving* (line 14) means:

(A) false

(B) blameless

(C) suspicious

(D) impeachable

(E) exemplary

Questions 26–32. Read the following poem carefully before choosing your answers.

## "Archaic Torso of Apollo"
by Rainer Marie Rilke; translated by Stephen Mitchell

*(1)* We cannot know his legendary head
with eyes like ripening fruit. And yet his torso
is still suffused with brilliance from inside,
like a lamp, in which his gaze, now turned to low,

*(5)* Gleams in all its power. Otherwise
the curved breast could not dazzle you so, nor could
a smile run through the placid hips and thighs

to that dark center where procreation flared.

*(9)* Otherwise this stone would seem defaced

*(10)* beneath the translucent cascade of the shoulders
and would not glisten like a wild beast's fur:

*(12)* would not, from all the borders of itself,
burst like a star: for here there is no place
that does not see you. You must change your life.

26. The author uses the simile in line 2 to:

(A) call attention to what is missing

(B) recall the features that made the subject legendary

(C) establish a tone of mourning

(D) amplify the expression of the statue

(E) indicate how the statue was perceived in its original state

27. The word *suffused* (line 3) means:

(A) penetrated

(B) filled

(C) spread

(D) released

(E) united

28. The use of the word *placid* (line 7) most likely suggests that

(A) The statue does not appear to have an intimidating demeanor.

(B) This portion of the statue does not contain the same degree of detail.

(C) This portion of the statue is absent, like the head.

(D) The sculptor was inattentive to this portion of the statue.

(E) The sculptor intended the statue to have a relaxed stance.

GO ON

29. The speaker compels a call to action in the last line because he believes:

   (A) people should emulate this experience daily.

   (B) people need to move away from the dullness of the everyday.

   (C) art possesses a transformative power.

   (D) one can be immortalized in art.

   (E) that viewing art can be a religious experience for some people.

30. The poem contains all of the following literary devices except:

   (A) simile

   (B) consonance

   (C) alliteration

   (D) imagery

   (E) personification

31. The tone of this poem could best be described as:

   (A) effervescent and wise

   (B) mature and enlightened

   (C) sensual and imaginative

   (D) appreciative and ethereal

   (E) awed and afraid

32. The light in this poem serves as a symbol for:

   (A) creativity

   (B) influence

   (C) deity

   (D) life

   (E) power

Questions 33–44. Read the following passage carefully before choosing your answers.

## Excerpt from "Miss Brill"
by Katherine Mansfield

*(1)* Oh, how fascinating it was! How she enjoyed it! How she loved sitting here, watching it all! It was like a play. It was exactly like a play. Who could believe the sky at the back wasn't painted? But it wasn't till a little brown dog trotted on solemn and then slowly trotted off, like a little "theatre" dog, a little dog that *(8)* had been drugged, that Miss Brill discovered what it was that made it so exciting. They were all on stage. They weren't only the audience, not only looking on; they were acting. Even she had a part and came every Sunday. No doubt somebody would have noticed if she hadn't been there; she was part of the performance after all. How strange *(16)* she'd never thought of it like that before! And yet it explained why she made such point of starting from home at just the same time each week—so as not to be late for the performance—and it also explained why she had a queer, shy feeling at telling her English pupils how she spent her Sunday afternoons. No wonder! Miss Brill nearly laughed out

*(24)* loud. She was on the stage. She thought of the old invalid gentleman to whom she read the newspaper four afternoons a week while he slept in the garden. She had got quite used to the frail head on the cotton pillow, the hollowed eyes, the open mouth and the high pinched nose. If he'd been dead she mightn't have noticed for weeks; she wouldn't have *(32)* minded. But suddenly he knew he was having the paper read to him by an actress! "An actress!" The old head lifted; two points of light quivered in the old eyes. "An actress— are ye?" And Miss Brill smoothed the newspaper as though it were the manuscript of her part and said gently; "Yes, I have been an actress for a long time."

*(40)* The band had been having a rest. Now they started again. And what they played was warm, sunny, yet there was just a faint chill—a something, what was it?—not sadness—no, not sadness—a something that made you want to sing. The tune lifted, lifted, the light shone; and it seemed to Miss Brill that in

*(47)* another moment all of them, all the whole company, would begin singing. The young ones, the laughing ones who were moving together, they would begin and the men's voices, very resolute and brave, would join them. And then she too, she too, and the others on the benches—they would come in

*(54)* with a kind of accompaniment—something low, that scarcely rose or fell, something so beautiful—moving... And Miss Brill's eyes filled with tears and she looked smiling at all the other members of the company. Yes, we understand, we understand, she thought—though what they understood she didn't know.

*(62)* Just at that moment a boy and girl came and sat down where the old couple had been. They were beautifully dressed; they were in love. The hero and heroine, of course, just arrived from his father's yacht. And still soundlessly singing, still with that trembling smile, Miss Brill prepared to listen.

*(69)* "No, not now," said the girl. "Not here, I can't."

"But why? Because of that stupid old thing at the end there?" asked the boy. "Why does she come here at all—who wants her? Why doesn't she keep her silly old mug at home?"

*(75)* "It's her fu-ur which is so funny," giggled the girl. "It's exactly like a fried whiting."

"Ah, be off with you!" said the boy in an angry whisper. Then: "Tell me, ma petite chère—"

"No, not here," said the girl. "Not yet."

*(81)* On her way home she usually bought a slice of honeycake at the baker's. It was her Sunday treat. Sometimes there was an almond in her slice, sometimes not. It made a great difference. If there was an almond

*(86)* it was like carrying home a tiny present–a surprise–something that might very well not have been there. She hurried on the almond Sundays and struck the match for the kettle in quite a dashing way.

*(91)* But to-day she passed the baker's by, climbed the stairs, went into the little dark room–her room like a cupboard–and sat down on the red eiderdown. She sat there for a long time. The box that the fur came out of was on

*(96)* the bed. She unclasped the necklet quickly; quickly, without looking, laid it inside. But when she put the lid on she thought she heard something crying.

33. The narrator speaks from which point of view?

   (A)  third person limited

   (B)  third person omniscient

   (C)  first person limited

   (D)  first person omniscient

   (E)  unreliable character

34. The author conveys the theme in part through

   (A)  characterization

   (B)  diction

   (C)  symbolism

   (D)  metaphor

   (E)  syntax

35. Miss Brill builds her life on:

   (A)  relaxation and enjoyment

   (B)  fantasy and self-deception

   (C)  service and solitude

   (D)  reality and honesty

   (E)  observation and evaluation

36. The fur most likely symbolizes

   (A)  the torn, tattered state of Miss Brill's life

   (B)  the state of Miss Brill's economic affairs

   (C)  the manner in which Miss Brill takes care of things

   (D)  the nurturing nature of Miss Brill

   (E)  the way others perceive Miss Brill

37. The word *invalid* in line 25 means:

    (A) untruthful

    (B) sickly

    (C) disposable

    (D) incorrect

    (E) paralyzed

38. Lines 40-68 reveal that the main character suffers from:

    (A) mental instability

    (B) hallucinations

    (C) wistfulness

    (D) active imagination

    (E) nostalgic episodes

39. The chief conflict in the passage occurs when Miss Brill:

    (A) removes the fur from the box

    (B) overhears the boy's comments

    (C) returns the fur to the box

    (D) hears unfamiliar cries

    (E) decides to go straight home

40. Based on this passage, the central theme is:

    (A) loneliness

    (B) aging

    (C) isolation

    (D) socialization

    (E) contentment

41. The reader can infer that Miss Brill did not go to the bakery because she felt:

    (A) content and tired

    (B) embarrassed and hurt

    (C) lonely and afraid

    (D) sad and forlorn

    (E) miserable and awkward

42. The last sentence of the story conveys:

    (A) the theme

    (B) Miss Brill's internal conflict

    (C) Miss Brill's delusion

    (D) a metaphor

    (E) allegorical representation

43. Overall, for readers, the shift in the story creates a sense of:

    (A) compassion

    (B) sadness

    (C) hopelessness

    (D) discouragement

    (E) pity

44. The purpose of the imagery in the story is to:

    (A) reveal how Miss Brill makes herself a part of the dramatic scenes of life

    (B) establish a tone of sympathy and authenticity

    (C) convey how Miss Brill derives rich enjoyment from her outings to the part.

    (D) contribute to the overall setting and sense of place

    (E) create the world in which Miss Brill derives pleasure

Questions 45-54. Read the following passage carefully before choosing your answers.

## Excerpt from "The Birth-Mark"
by Nathaniel Hawthorne

(1) In the latter part of the last century there lived a man of science, an eminent proficient in every branch of natural philosophy, who not long before our story opens had made experience of a spiritual affinity more attractive than any chemical one. He had left his laboratory to the care of an assistant, cleared his fine countenance from the

(9) furnace smoke, washed the stain of acids from his fingers, and persuaded a beautiful woman to become his wife. In those days when the comparatively recent discovery of electricity and other kindred mysteries of Nature seemed to open paths into the region of miracle, it was not unusual for the love of science to rival the love of woman in its depth and absorbing energy. The higher

(18) intellect, the imagination, the spirit, and even the heart might all find their congenial aliment in pursuits which, as some of their ardent votaries believed, would ascend from one step of powerful intelligence to another, until the philosopher should lay his hand on the secret of creative force and perhaps make new worlds for himself. We know not whether Aylmer possessed this degree of

(27) faith in man's ultimate control over Nature. He had devoted himself, however, too unreservedly to scientific studies ever to be weaned from them by any second passion. His love for his young wife might prove the stronger of the two; but it could only be by intertwining itself with his love of science, and uniting the strength of the latter to his own.

(36) Such a union accordingly took place, and was attended with truly remarkable consequences and a deeply impressive moral. One day, very soon after their marriage, Aylmer sat gazing at his wife with a trouble in his countenance that grew stronger until he spoke.

(43) "Georgiana," said he, "has it never occurred to you that the mark upon your cheek might be removed?"

(46) "No, indeed," said she, smiling; but perceiving the seriousness of his manner, she blushed deeply. "To tell you the truth it has been so often called a charm that I was simple enough to imagine it might be so."

(51) "Ah, upon another face perhaps it might," replied her husband; "but never on yours. No, dearest Georgiana, you came so nearly perfect from the hand of Nature that this slightest possible defect, which we hesitate whether to term a defect or a beauty, shocks me, as being the visible mark of earthly imperfection."

(59) "Shocks you, my husband!" cried Georgiana, deeply hurt; at first reddening with momentary anger, but then bursting into tears. "Then why did you take me from my mother's side? You cannot love what shocks you!"

(65) To explain this conversation it must be mentioned that in the centre of Georgiana's left cheek there was a singular mark, deeply interwoven, as it were, with the texture and substance of her face. In the usual state of her complexion—a healthy though delicate bloom—the mark wore a tint of deeper crimson, which imperfectly defined its shape amid the surrounding rosiness. When she

(74) blushed it gradually became more indistinct, and finally vanished amid the triumphant rush of blood that bathed the whole cheek with its brilliant glow. But if any shifting motion caused her to turn pale there was the mark again, a crimson stain upon the snow, in what Aylmer sometimes deemed an almost fearful distinctness. Its shape bore not a little similarity to the human hand, though of the smallest pygmy size.

(84) Georgiana's lovers were wont to say that some fairy at her birth hour had laid her tiny hand upon the infant's cheek, and left this impress there in token of the magic endowments that were to give her such sway over all hearts. Many a desperate swain would have risked life for the privilege of pressing his lips to the mysterious hand. It must not be concealed, however, that

(93) the impression wrought by this fairy sign manual varied exceedingly, according to the difference of temperament in the beholders. Some fastidious persons—but they were exclusively of her own sex—affirmed that the bloody hand, as they chose to call it, quite destroyed the effect of Georgiana's beauty, and rendered her countenance even hideous. But it would be as reasonable to say that one

(102) of those small blue stains which sometimes occur in the purest statuary marble would convert the Eve of Powers to a monster. Masculine observers, if the birthmark did not heighten their admiration, contented themselves with wishing it away, that the world might possess one living specimen of ideal loveliness without the semblance of a flaw. After his marriage—for he thought little or nothing of the matter before— Aylmer discovered that this was the case with himself.

(114) Had she been less beautiful,—if Envy's self could have found aught else to sneer at,—he might have felt his affection heightened by the prettiness of this mimic hand, now vaguely portrayed, now lost, now stealing forth again and glimmering to and fro with every pulse of emotion that throbbed within her heart; but seeing her otherwise so perfect, he found this one defect grow more and more

(123) intolerable with every moment of their united lives. It was the fatal flaw of humanity which Nature, in one shape or another, stamps ineffaceably on all her productions, either to imply that they are temporary and finite, or that their perfection must be wrought by toil and pain. The crimson hand expressed the ineludible gripe in which mortality clutches the highest and purest of earthly mould, degrading them into kindred with

(132) the lowest, and even with the very brutes, like whom their visible frames return to dust. In this manner, selecting it as the symbol of his wife's liability to sin, sorrow, decay, and death, Aylmer's sombre imagination was not long in rendering the birthmark a frightful object, causing him more trouble and horror than ever Georgiana's beauty, whether of soul or sense, had given him delight.

45. The word *countenance* (line 8) means:

    (A) demeanor

    (B) gait

    (C) opposition to

    (D) face

    (E) wealth

46. The reader can infer that Georgiana never had her birthmark removed because:

    (A) She innocently believed it was charming.

    (B) Her mother's family would have disapproved.

    (C) Others had complimented her on it.

    (D) She did not support medical surgeries.

    (E) She could not afford it.

47. Lines 81-113 serve all of the following purposes except to:

    (A) describe the physical appearance of Georgiana

    (B) explain why others saw her as beautiful

    (C) relate why her beauty was seen as tainted

    (D) provide insight into Georgiana's self-concept

    (E) state how her husband managed to see her as beautiful

48. What does the birthmark represent to Alymer?

    (A) nature's fatal flaw

    (B) Georgiana's humanity

    (C) his desire towards perfection

    (D) Georgiana's desires

    (E) a lack of beauty

49. The redness of the birthmark most likely symbolizes:

    (A) new life

    (B) passion

    (C) sexuality

    (D) maturity

    (E) experience

50. The one point of the passage that contains an inconsistent point of view is:

    (A) *In the latter part of the last century there lived a man of science…*

    (B) *We know not whether Aylmer possessed this degree of faith in man's ultimate control over Nature.*

    (C) *His love for his young wife might prove the stronger of the two...*

    (D) *Masculine observers, if the birthmark did not heighten their admiration...*

    (E) *If Envy's self could have found aught else to sneer at...*

51. This passage most likely belongs to the genre of:

    (A) parables

    (B) Gothic fiction

    (C) dark Romanticism

    (D) historical fiction

    (E) Romanticism

52. The diction in the first paragraph contributes to a writing style that is:

    (A) grand

    (B) laborious

    (C) dense

    (D) formal

    (E) opulent

53. Which of the following statements is not true about Georgiana, based on this passage?

    (A) She is the archetype of the naïve young wife.

    (B) She bases her self-worth in external appearances.

    (C) She is not afraid to challenge her husband.

    (D) She trusts her husband.

    (E) She is not weak.

54. One can infer that Alymer's greatest character flaw is:

    (A) pride

    (B) ambition

    (C) greed

    (D) jealousy

    (E) gluttony

55. The tone of the passage is:

    (A) condescending and judgmental

    (B) grandiose and proper

    (C) dark and foreboding

    (D) heavy and intense

    (E) didactic and moralistic

GO ON

# Section II: One Hour

This section includes selections from literary works, followed by questions that will ask you to address their form, content, and style. After reading each selection, craft a well-written essay that responds to the question.

Poetry: The following poem is a villanelle, a form having strict rules of rhyme, meter, and repetition. Read the poem carefully. Then write a well-organized essay in which you analyze how the formal elements of the poem contribute to its meaning.

## "Do Not Go Gentle Into That Good Night"
### by Dylan Thomas

(1) Do not go gentle into that good night,
Old age should burn and rave at close of day;
Rage, rage against the dying of the light.

(4) Though wise men at their end know dark is right,
Because their words had forked no lightning they
Do not go gentle into that good night.

(7) Good men, the last wave by, crying how bright
Their frail deeds might have danced in a green bay,
Rage, rage against the dying of the light.

(10) Wild men who caught and sang the sun in flight,
And learn, too late, they grieved it on its way,
Do not go gentle into that good night.

(13) Grave men, near death, who see with blinding sight
Blind eyes could blaze like meteors and be gay,
Rage, rage against the dying of the light.

(16) And you, my father, there on that sad height,
Curse, bless, me now with your fierce tears, I pray.
Do not go gentle into that good night.
Rage, rage against the dying of the light.

Prose: After reading the following passage, write a well-organized essay that discusses the conflict of the unreliable narrator.

## "The Yellow Wallpaper"
### by Charlotte Perkins Gilman

(1) We have been here two weeks, and I haven't felt like writing before, since that first day.

I am sitting by the window now, up in this atrocious nursery, and there is nothing to hinder my writing as much as I please, save lack of strength.

(7) John is away all day, and even some nights when his cases are serious.

I am glad my case is not serious!

(10) But these nervous troubles are dreadfully depressing.

John does not know how much I really suffer.

(13) He knows there is no reason to suffer, and that satisfies him.

Of course it is only nervousness. It does weigh on me so not to do my duty in any way!

(18) I meant to be such a help to John, such a real rest and comfort, and here I am a comparative burden already!

Nobody would believe what an effort it is to do what little I am able—to dress and entertain, and order things.

(24) It is fortunate Mary is so good with the baby. Such a dear baby!

(26) And yet I cannot be with him, it makes me so nervous.

I suppose John never was nervous in his life. He laughs at me so about this wall-paper!

At first he meant to repaper the room, but afterwards he said that I was letting it get the better of me, and that nothing was worse for a nervous patient than to give way to such fancies.

(35) He said that after the wall-paper was changed it would be the heavy bedstead, and then the barred windows, and then that gate at the head of the stairs, and so on.

"You know the place is doing you good," he said, "and really, dear, I don't care to renovate the house just for a three months' rental."

(42) "Then do let us go downstairs," I said, "there are such pretty rooms there."

Then he took me in his arms and called me a blessed little goose, and said he would go down to the cellar, if I wished, and have it whitewashed into the bargain.

But he is right enough about the beds and windows and things.

(50) It is an airy and comfortable room as any one need wish, and, of course, I would not be so silly as to make him uncomfortable just for a whim.

I'm really getting quite fond of the big room, all but that horrid paper.

Out of one window I can see the garden, those mysterious deepshaded arbors, the riotous old-fashioned flowers, and bushes and gnarly trees.

(60) Out of another I get a lovely view of the bay and a little private wharf belonging to the estate. There is a beautiful shaded lane that runs down there from the house. I always fancy I see people walking in these numerous paths and arbors, but John has cautioned me not to give way to fancy in the least. He says that with my imaginative power and habit of story-making, a nervous weakness like mine is sure to lead to all manner of excited fancies, and that I ought to use my will and good sense to check the tendency. So I try.

(72) I think sometimes that if I were only well enough to write a little it would relieve the press of ideas and rest me.

But I find I get pretty tired when I try.

(76) It is so discouraging not to have any advice and companionship about my work. When I get really well, John says we will ask Cousin Henry and Julia down for a long visit; but he says he would as soon put fireworks in my pillow-case as to let me have those stimulating people about now.

I wish I could get well faster.

(84) But I must not think about that. This paper looks to me as if it knew what a vicious influence it had!

There is a recurrent spot where the pattern lolls like a broken neck and two bulbous eyes stare at you upside down.

(90) I get positively angry with the impertinence of it and the everlastingness. Up and down and sideways they crawl, and those absurd, unblinking eyes are everywhere There is one place where two breaths didn't match, and the eyes go all up and down the line, one a little higher than the other.

(97) I never saw so much expression in an inanimate thing before, and we all know how much expression they have! I used to lie awake as a child and get more entertainment and terror out of blank walls and plain furniture than most children could find in a toy-store.

(104) I remember what a kindly wink the knobs of our big, old bureau used to have, and there was one chair that always seemed like a strong friend.

I used to feel that if any of the other things looked too fierce I could always hop into that chair and be safe.

(111) The furniture in this room is no worse than inharmonious, however, for we had to bring it all from downstairs. I suppose when this was used as a playroom they had to take the nursery things out, and no wonder! I never saw such ravages as the children have made here.

*(118)* The wall-paper, as I said before, is torn off in spots, and it sticketh closer than a brother—they must have had perseverance as well as hatred.

Then the floor is scratched and gouged and splintered, the plaster itself is dug out here and there, and this great heavy bed which is all we found in the room, looks as if it had been through the wars.

*(127)* But I don't mind it a bit—only the paper.

There comes John's sister. Such a dear girl as she is, and so careful of me! I must not let her find me writing.

She is a perfect and enthusiastic housekeeper, and hopes for no better profession. I verily believe she thinks it is the writing which made me sick!

*(135)* But I can write when she is out, and see her a long way off from these windows.

There is one that commands the road, a lovely shaded winding road, and one that just looks off over the country. A lovely country, too, full of great elms and velvet meadows.

*(141)* This wall-paper has a kind of sub-pattern in a, different shade, a particularly irritating one, for you can only see it in certain lights, and not clearly then.

But in the places where it isn't faded and where the sun is just so--I can see a strange, provoking, formless sort of figure, that seems to skulk about behind that silly and conspicuous front design.

There's sister on the stairs!

Open Answer: According to the Dalai Lama, "even when a person has all of life's comforts—good food, good shelter, a companion—he or she can still become unhappy when encountering a tragic situation." Select a novel or a play in which a character who has all of "life's comforts" encounters tragedy. Then write an essay in which you explain how the suffering brought about by the tragedy surpasses the character's comforts.

# Answer Key (Practice Test Two)

| | | | | | |
|---|---|---|---|---|---|
| 1. | (B) | 20. | (E) | 39. | (B) |
| 2. | (A) | 21. | (D) | 40. | (A) |
| 3. | (C) | 22. | (B) | 41. | (B) |
| 4. | (E) | 23. | (B) | 42. | (C) |
| 5. | (B) | 24. | (B) | 43. | (A) |
| 6. | (D) | 25. | (B) | 44. | (A) |
| 7. | (D) | 26. | (D) | 45. | (D) |
| 8. | (B) | 27. | (B) | 46. | (A) |
| 9. | (A) | 28. | (E) | 47. | (D) |
| 10. | (B) | 29. | (C) | 48. | (B) |
| 11. | (C) | 30. | (E) | 49. | (C) |
| 12. | (B) | 31. | (B) | 50. | (B) |
| 13. | (E) | 32. | (D) | 51. | (C) |
| 14. | (E) | 33. | (A) | 52. | (A) |
| 15. | (C) | 34. | (C) | 53. | (A) |
| 16. | (B) | 35. | (B) | 54. | (B) |
| 17. | (D) | 36. | (A) | 55. | (E) |
| 18. | (A) | 37. | (B) | | |
| 19. | (E) | 38. | (B) | | |

# ten

# PRACTICE TEST THREE

## Section I: One Hour

This section includes selections from literary works, followed by questions about their form, content, and style. After reading each selection, choose the best answer to each question.

Questions 1–14. Read the following poem carefully before choosing your answers.

### "Sonnet 116"
### by William Shakespeare

(1) Let me not to the marriage of true minds
Admit impediments. Love is not love
Which alters when it alteration finds,
Or bends with the remover to remove:
(5) O no; it is an ever-fixed mark,
That looks on tempests, and is never shaken;
It is the star to every wandering bark,
Whose worth's unknown, although his height be taken.

(9) Love's not Time's fool, though rosy lips and cheeks
Within his bending sickle's compass come;
Love alters not with his brief hours and weeks,
But bears it out even to the edge of doom.
(13) If this be error and upon me proved,
I never writ, nor no man ever loved.

1. The word *impediments* in line 2 means:

   (A) distractions
   (B) hardships
   (C) hindrances
   (D) pathways
   (E) conditions

2. The main literary device used in the first quatrain is:

   (A) repetition
   (B) assonance
   (C) alliteration
   (D) consonance
   (E) metaphor

3. The word *bark* (line 7) in context means:

   (A) noise

   (B) soul

   (C) nomad

   (D) boat

   (E) mongrel

4. The *bending sickle* in the third quatrain is a reference to:

   (A) pastoral equipment

   (B) death

   (C) contagious disease

   (D) the grim reaper

   (E) judgment day

5. In line 9, the speaker asserts that:

   (A) Love does not know the bounds of time.

   (B) Love is not reserved only for the young.

   (C) True love does not change with time.

   (D) Love does not pander to time.

   (E) True love never ages.

6. The author uses all of the following literary devices in the third quatrain except:

   (A) personification

   (B) consonance

   (C) hyperbole

   (D) alliteration

   (E) allegory

7. The purpose of the couplet is to:

   (A) provide a dramatic challenge to the reader

   (B) defend the speaker's stance

   (C) reveal a bold conclusion

   (D) end with a legalistic and logical statement

   (E) reveal the speaker's confidence in his beliefs

8. What does the author mean by *whose worth's unknown, although his height be taken*?

   (A) We do not appreciate the value of the guiding force of love.

   (B) There is simply no way to estimate the worth of love in our lives.

   (C) True love can lift us to the pinnacle of developmental heights.

   (D) We take advantage of love with appreciating it.

   (E) The height of love leads us to become unappreciative.

9. *The star to every wandering bark* is referring to what?

   (A) the sun

   (B) a star

   (C) the north star

   (D) love

   (E) a lighthouse

10. The nautical images serve as:

    (A) details that reveal tone

    (B) personification of a lost ship

    (C) symbols of love leading us through life

    (D) contrasts with the roughness of the sea

    (E) metaphors of what plagues relationships

11. The speaker's point of view is that love is:

    (A) idealistic and transcendent

    (B) conforming and conventional

    (C) obedient and subservient

    (D) holy and sacramental

    (E) intellectual and equal

12. The author's message is that:

    (A) Love requires forgiveness above all else.

    (B) The hallmark of true love is persistence.

    (C) Regardless of circumstances, love prevails.

    (D) Marriage is best reserved for those of like mind.

    (E) Nobody has ever truly loved before.

13. Which of the following statements offers the best paraphrase of lines 1 and 2?

   (A) Do not allow me to give reasons why two like-minded people cannot marry.

   (B) Perfect love is a partnership between two thinking, considerate individuals.

   (C) A true marriage is without fault.

   (D) Faultless love begins with friendship.

   (E) Troubles occur when marriages begin with ill-matched partners.

14. What is the result of the enjambment between the first two lines?

   (A) It permits further emphasis on the word *admit*.

   (B) It does not even allow *impediments* to enter the first line.

   (C) It presents the idea of obstruction in the second line.

   (D) It keeps the introductory concept pure from impediment.

   (E) It maintains the iambic pentameter.

Questions 15–26. Read the following poem carefully before choosing your answers.

## "If"

### by Rudyard Kipling

*(1)* If you can keep your head when all about you
Are losing theirs and blaming it on you;
If you can trust yourself when all men doubt you,
But make allowance for their doubting too:
If you can wait and not be tired by waiting,
Or, being lied about, don't deal in lies,
Or being hated don't give way to hating,
And yet don't look too good, nor talk too wise;

*(9)* If you can dream—and not make dreams your master;
If you can think—and not make thoughts your aim,
If you can meet with Triumph and Disaster
And treat those two impostors just the same:.
If you can bear to hear the truth you've spoken
Twisted by knaves to make a trap for fools,
Or watch the things you gave your life to, broken,
And stoop and build'em up with worn-out tools;

*(17)* If you can make one heap of all your winnings
And risk it on one turn of pitch-and-toss,
And lose, and start again at your beginnings,
And never breathe a word about your loss:
If you can force your heart and nerve and sinew
To serve your turn long after they are gone,
And so hold on when there is nothing in you
Except the Will which says to them: "Hold on!"

*(25)* If you can talk with crowds and keep your virtue,
Or walk with Kings—nor lose the common touch,
If neither foes nor loving friends can hurt you,
If all men count with you, but none too much:
If you can fill the unforgiving minute
With sixty seconds' worth of distance run,
Yours is the Earth and everything that's in it,
And—which is more—you'll be a Man, my son!

GO ON

15. What does speaker suggest in these lines: *If you can dream—and not make dreams your master/If you can think—and not make thoughts your aim*?

    (A) Idealizing what you dream and think about causes stagnation.

    (B) Thinking too much causes confusion.

    (C) Trying to impress others with your intellect is futile.

    (D) Do not fall victim to figments of the imagination.

    (E) Moderation is the key to success.

16. All of the following concepts are personified in the poem except:

    (A) dreams

    (B) triumph

    (C) disaster

    (D) will

    (E) failure

17. The speaker warns against the error of:

    (A) self-righteousness

    (B) arrogance

    (C) unawareness

    (D) redundancy

    (E) wildness

18. The tone of the poem can best be described as:

    (A) didactic and hopeful

    (B) moralistic and encouraging

    (C) warm and sentimental

    (D) inspiring and noble

    (E) nostalgic and trusting

19. The repetition of the word *if*:

    (A) creates a sense of urgency within the poem

    (B) supports the rhyme and meter

    (C) establishes lyricism and tension

    (D) forces anticipation

    (E) surrounds the poem with ennui

20. What does the speaker mean by *unforgiving minute*?

    (A) Time waits for nobody.

    (B) Time passes at immeasurable speeds.

    (C) You cannot retract time.

    (D) Time is the one constant.

    (E) Time shows no mercy.

21. The message of the poem can be stated best as:

    (A) Living honorably is possible by choosing correctly.

    (B) Replicating the actions of your father ensures you will become like him.

    (C) It is necessary to follow certain rules and behaviors to reach adulthood.

    (D) It is possible to grow old without ever having reached full maturity.

    (E) There is a delicate balance to living well.

22. The word *knaves* (line 22) refers to:

    (A) miscreants

    (B) servants

    (C) innocents

    (D) saints

    (E) heroes

23. The characteristic tone of the author's style is one of:

    (A) motivation

    (B) contingency

    (C) doubt

    (D) paradox

    (E) exhortation

24. The poem's central idea about success is that it comes from:

    (A) willingness

    (B) self-control

    (C) obedience

    (D) virtue

    (E) patience

25. It can be inferred that the speaker believes masculinity requires all of the following qualities except:

    (A) stoicism

    (B) reserve

    (C) heroic deeds

    (D) prudence

    (E) wisdom

26. The word *sinew* (line 21) refers to:

    (A) marrow

    (B) valor

    (C) muscle

    (D) tendon

    (E) power

Questions 27–36. Read the following poem carefully before choosing your answers.

## "Conversion"
### by Jean Toomer

*(1)*  African Guardian of Souls,
      Drunk with rum,
      Feasting on strange cassava,
      Yielding to new words and a weak palabra
*(5)*  Of a white-faced sardonic god—
      Grins, cries
      Amen,
      Shouts hosanna.

27. The genre that best fits this poem would be:

    (A) farce

    (B) carpe diem

    (C) allegory

    (D) ode

    (E) address

28. The word *cassava* on line 3 refers to:

    (A) a type of rum

    (B) the food of the Africans

    (C) the food of the white-faced god

    (D) a meal

    (E) a plant

29. The poem best addresses the topic of:

    (A) a lost identity

    (B) religious experience

    (C) racial relations

    (D) intercultural exchanges

    (E) worship ceremonies

30. Line 8 reveals a:

    (A) transformation

    (B) proclamation

    (C) conversion

    (D) statement of praise

    (E) ownership

31. The connotation of *yielding* (line 4) implies:

    (A) producing

    (B) submitting

    (C) pliability

    (D) furnishing

    (E) resisting

32. The enjambment in line 6 :

    (A) creates a stark emotional contrast

    (B) reveals the effect of the cassava

    (C) establishes a sense of speed

    (D) evokes sympathy

    (E) serves as a parallel to previous events

33. The speaker's message can best be summarized as:

(A) The loss of traditions results in a lost and confused identity.

(B) Religious experiences are necessary for uplifting our spirit.

(C) Ingesting unknown substances results in poor decision-making.

(D) A range of emotions must be experienced in order to obtain wisdom.

(E) Changing the tenets of a belief system is beneficial to development.

34. The author characterizes the *African Guardian of Souls* as:

(A) drunk and hungry

(B) elementary and naive

(C) untamed and liberated

(D) humble and revered

(E) protective and transcendent

Questions 35–42. Read the following passage carefully before choosing your answers.

## "Gooseberries"
### Anton Chekhov

(1) They went to the house. And only when the lamp was lit in the large drawing-room up-stairs, and Bourkin and Ivan Ivanich, dressed in silk dressing-gowns and warm slippers, lounged in chairs, and Aliokhin himself, washed and brushed, in a new frock coat, paced up and down evidently delighting in the warmth and cleanliness

(9) and dry clothes and slippers, and pretty Pelagueya, noiselessly tripping over the carpet and smiling sweetly, brought in tea and jam on a tray, only then did Ivan Ivanich begin his story, and it was as though he was being listened to not only by Bourkin and Aliokhin, but also by the old and young ladies and the officer who looked down so staidly and tranquilly from the golden frames.

(18) "We are two brothers," he began, "I, Ivan Ivanich, and Nicholai Ivanich, two years younger. I went in for study and became a veterinary surgeon, while Nicholai was at the Exchequer Court when he was nineteen. Our father, Tchimsha-Himalaysky, was a cantonist, but he died with an officer's rank and left us his title of nobility and a small

(26) estate. After his death the estate went to pay his debts. However, we spent our childhood there in the country. We were just like peasant's children, spent days and nights in the fields and the woods, minded the horses, barked the lime-trees, fished, and so

(32) on... And you know once a man has fished, or watched the thrushes hovering in flocks over the village in the bright, cool, autumn days, he can never really be a townsman, and to the day of his death he will be drawn to the country. My brother pined away in the

(38) Exchequer. Years passed and he sat in the same place, wrote out the same documents, and thought of one thing, how to get back to the country. And little by little his distress became a definite disorder, a fixed idea—to buy a small farm somewhere by the bank of a river or a lake.

(45) "He was a good fellow and I loved him, but I never sympathised with the desire to shut oneself up on one's own farm. It is a common saying that a man needs only six feet of land. But surely a corpse wants that, not a man. And I hear that our intellectuals have a longing for the land and want to acquire farms. But it all comes down to the six feet

(53) of land. To leave town, and the struggle and the swim of life, and go and hide yourself in a farmhouse is not life—it is egoism, laziness; it is a kind of monasticism, but monasticism without action. A man needs, not six feet of land, not a farm, but the whole earth, all Nature, where in full liberty he can display all the properties and qualities of the free spirit.

(61) "My brother Nicholai, sitting in his office, would dream of eating his own schi, with its savoury smell floating across the farmyard; and of eating out in the open air, and of sleeping in the sun, and of sitting for hours together on a seat by the gate and gazing at the fields and the forest. Books on agriculture

(68) and the hints in almanacs were his joy, his favourite spiritual food; and he liked reading newspapers, but only the advertisements of land to be sold, so many acres of arable and grass land, with a farmhouse, river, garden, mill, and mill-pond. And he would dream of garden-walls, flowers, fruits, nests, carp in the

(75) pond, don't you know, and all the rest of it. These fantasies of his used to vary according to the advertisements he found, but somehow there was always a gooseberry-bush in every one. Not a house, not a romantic spot could he imagine without its gooseberry-bush.

(81) "'Country life has its advantages,' he used to say. 'You sit on the veranda drinking tea and your ducklings swim on the pond, and everything smells good. . . and there are gooseberries.'

(86) "He used to draw out a plan of his estate and always the same things were shown on it: (a) Farmhouse, (b) cottage, (c) vegetable garden, (d) gooseberry-bush. He used to live meagerly and never had enough to eat and drink, dressed God knows how, exactly like a

(92) beggar, and always saved and put his money into the bank. He was terribly stingy. It used to hurt me to see him, and I used to give him money to go away for a holiday, but he would put that away, too. Once a man gets a fixed idea, there's nothing to be done.

(98) "Years passed; he was transferred to another province. He completed his fortieth year and was still reading advertisements in the papers and saving up his money. Then I heard he was married. Still with the same idea of buying a farmhouse with a gooseberry-bush,

(104) he married an elderly, ugly widow, not out of any feeling for her, but because she had money. With her he still lived stingily, kept her half-starved, and put the money into the bank in his own name. She had been the wife of a postmaster and was used to good

(110) living, but with her second husband she did not even have enough black bread; she pined away in her new life, and in three years or so gave up her soul to God. And my brother never for a moment thought himself to blame for her death. Money, like vodka, can play queer tricks with a man. Once in our town a

(117) merchant lay dying. Before his death he asked for some honey, and he ate all his notes and scrip with the honey so that nobody should get it. Once I was examining a herd of cattle at a station and a horse-jobber fell under the engine, and his foot was cut off. We carried

(123) him into the waiting-room, with the blood pouring down—a terrible business—and all the while he kept asking anxiously for his foot; he had twenty-five roubles in his boot and did not want to lose them."

"Keep to your story," said Bourkin.

(129) "After the death of his wife," Ivan Ivanich continued, after a long pause, "my brother began to look out for an estate. Of course you may search for five years, and even then buy a pig in a poke. Through an agent my brother Nicholai raised a mortgage and bought three hundred acres with a farmhouse, a cottage,

(136) and a park, but there was no orchard, no gooseberry-bush, no duck-pond; there was a river but the water in it was coffee-coloured because the estate lay between a brick-yard and a gelatine factory. But my brother Nicholai was not worried about that; he ordered twenty gooseberry-bushes and settled down to a country life.

(144) "Last year I paid him a visit. I thought I'd go and see how things were with him. In his letters my brother called his estate Tchimbarshov Corner, or Himalayskoe. I arrived at Himalayskoe in the afternoon. It was hot. There were ditches, fences, hedges, rows of young fir-trees, trees everywhere, and

(151) there was no telling how to cross the yard or where to put your horse. I went to the house and was met by a red-haired dog, as fat as a pig. He tried to bark but felt too lazy. Out of the kitchen came the cook, barefooted, and also as fat as a pig, and said that the master was having his afternoon rest. I went in to my brother and found him sitting on his bed

*(159)* with his knees covered with a blanket; he looked old, stout, flabby; his cheeks, nose, and lips were pendulous. I half expected him to grunt like a pig.

35. This story is best characterized as a(n):

    (A) allegory

    (B) frame story

    (C) historical fiction

    (D) journalistic account

    (E) morality play

36. The author equates gooseberries with:

    (A) luxury

    (B) opulence

    (C) hunger

    (D) poverty

    (E) satisfaction

37. The author's message is that:

    (A) It is the responsibility of man to alleviate suffering in life.

    (B) Man's greatest desire is to be happy.

    (C) Material possessions do not equate contentedness.

    (D) Societal standards have led to widespread feelings of inadequacy.

    (E) It is prudent to be opportunistic.

38. Line 128 contains an example of:

    (A) axiom

    (B) metaphor

    (C) simile

    (D) oxymoron

    (E) trope

*(163)* "We embraced and shed a tear of joy and also of sadness to think that we had once been young, but were now both going grey and nearing death. He dressed and took me to see his estate."

39. The author characterizes Nicholai as:

    (A) idealistic and sacrificial

    (B) hopeful and stubborn

    (C) materialistic and depressed

    (D) rude and stingy

    (E) delusional and inane

40. The story is told from the _____ point of view:

    (A) first-person limited

    (B) first-person omniscient

    (C) second person

    (D) third-person limited

    (E) third-person omniscient

41. It can be inferred that Nicholai holds onto the dream of a farm with gooseberry bushes because:

    (A) He longs to escape from reality.

    (B) He desires a simple way of living.

    (C) He hopes to re-create his childhood.

    (D) He wishes to re-establish the happiness of his youth.

    (E) He feels that it will bring him better health.

42. The images in lines 154–162 connote:

    (A) complacency

    (B) vigilance

    (C) reprieve

    (D) diligence

    (E) laziness

43. When the speaker describes their youthful activities in lines 28–32, it indicates that:

(A) Their childhood was filled with nature.

(B) In spite of being peasant's children, they enjoyed great happiness.

(C) There was a lingering resentment over being a peasant's child.

(D) There were bigger reasons for wanting farm life in adulthood.

(E) The toys of nature were preferred to manmade playthings.

44. The speaker's claim that ...*my brother never for a moment thought himself to blame for her death. Money, like vodka, can play queer tricks with a man* (lines 113–116) is used to imply what about Nicholai?

(A) He felt great remorse over his wife's death.

(B) He later developed a drinking problem.

(C) He was absent-minded.

(D) He was responsible for his wife's death.

(E) He had hated his wife.

45. When the speaker explains that *A man needs, not six feet of land, not a farm, but the whole earth, all Nature, where in full liberty he can display all the properties and qualities of the free spirit* (lines 57–60), the reader understands that:

(A) Man will continue to want to expand his ownership of nature until he owns everything.

(B) Fulfilling the dream of a pastoral life is not what is necessary for freedom.

(C) Spending time in nature allows man to develop freely.

(D) Even the entirety of the earth is not enough for man to feel free.

(E) Man's liberation cannot be contained by the grave.

46. The primary literary device the author employs is:

(A) narration

(B) visual imagery

(C) symbolism

(D) irony

(E) characterization

Questions 47–55. Read the following passage and carefully review the questions that follow.

## Excerpt from "A Garden Party"
### Katherine Mansfield

(1) It was just growing dusky as Laura shut their garden gates. A big dog ran by like a shadow. The road gleamed white, and down below in the hollow the little cottages were in deep shade. How quiet it seemed after the afternoon. Here she was going down the hill to somewhere where a man lay dead, and she couldn't realize it. Why couldn't she? She

(9) stopped a minute. And it seemed to her that kisses, voices, tinkling spoons, laughter, the smell of crushed grass were somehow inside her. She had no room for anything else. How strange! She looked up at the pale sky, and all she thought was, "Yes, it was the most successful party."

(16) Now the broad road was crossed. The lane began, smoky and dark. Women in shawls

(18) and men's tweed caps hurried by. Men hung over the palings; the children played in the doorways. A low hum came from the mean little cottages. In some of them there was a flicker of light, and a shadow, crab-like, moved across the window. Laura bent her

(24) head and hurried on. She wished now she had put on a coat. How her frock shone! And the big hat with the velvet streamer - if only it was another hat! Were the people looking at her? They must be. It was a mistake to have come; she knew all along it was a mistake. Should she go back even now?

(31) No, too late. This was the house. It must be. A dark knot of people stood outside. Beside the gate an old, old woman with a crutch sat in a chair, watching. She had her feet on a

(35) newspaper. The voices stopped as Laura drew near. The group parted. It was as though she was expected, as though they had known she was coming here.

47. The passage contains all of the following literary devices except:

    (A) sensory details

    (B) visual imagery

    (C) simile

    (D) metaphor

    (E) symbolism

48. When the speaker says that *kisses, voices, tinkling spoons, laughter, the smell of crushed grass were somehow inside her. She had no room for anything else* (lines 9–12), she reveals that the character is:

    (A) consumed by the joy of the party

    (B) in denial about the man's death

    (C) confused about where she is going

    (D) planning to host a garden party soon

    (E) walking home from the garden party

49. The first paragraph demonstrates the author's use of:

    (A) metaphor

    (B) simile

    (C) allegory

    (D) imagery

    (E) diction

50. The move downhill symbolizes:

    (A) change from the wealthy to the lower class

    (B) barriers towards acceptance

    (C) a shift in the plot line

    (D) the character's personal decline

    (E) the character's personal growth

51. The final paragraph in the passage mostly indicates that Laura:

    (A) is welcome at her destination

    (B) is the subject of gossip

    (C) is received skeptically

    (D) tries too hard to be accepted

    (E) does not wear the correct apparel for the setting

52. As used in line 20, the word *mean* most nearly means:

    (A) angry

    (B) unkind

    (C) intentional

    (D) shabby

    (E) normal

53. The controlling literary element in the passage is:

    (A) narrator

    (B) plot

    (C) setting

    (D) conflict

    (E) theme

54. The reader can infer from the line *She wished now she had put on a coat* (lines 24–25) that Laura:

    (A) is primarily concerned with outward appearances

    (B) feels embarrassed by her attire

    (C) is affected dramatically by changes in weather

    (D) wishes that she could disguise herself

    (E) feels uncomfortable with her circumstances

55. The word *hollow* on line 4 refers to:

    (A) a hole

    (B) an insignificance

    (C) a depression

    (D) a trough

    (E) a small valley

# Section II: One Hour

**Directions: This section includes selections from literary works, followed by questions that will ask you to address their form, content, and style. After reading each selection, craft a well-written essay that responds to the question.**

Poetry: Read the following poem carefully, paying particular attention to the physical intensity of the language. Then write a well-organized essay in which you explain how the poet conveys not just a literal description of the birches, but a deeper understanding of the whole experience. You may wish to include analysis of such elements as diction, imagery, metaphor, rhyme, rhythm, and form.

### "Birches"
### by Robert Frost

(1)  When I see birches bend to left and right
Across the lines of straighter darker trees,
I like to think some boy's been swinging them.
But swinging doesn't bend them down to stay.
(5)  Ice-storms do that. Often you must have seen them
Loaded with ice a sunny winter morning
After a rain. They click upon themselves
As the breeze rises, and turn many-coloured
As the stir cracks and crazes their enamel.
(10)  Soon the sun's warmth makes them shed crystal shells
Shattering and avalanching on the snow-crust
Such heaps of broken glass to sweep away
You'd think the inner dome of heaven had fallen.
They are dragged to the withered bracken by the load,
(15)  And they seem not to break; though once they are bowed
So low for long, they never right themselves:
You may see their trunks arching in the woods
Years afterwards, trailing their leaves on the ground,
Like girls on hands and knees that throw their hair
(20)  Before them over their heads to dry in the sun.
But I was going to say when Truth broke in
With all her matter-of-fact about the ice-storm,

(23)  I should prefer to have some boy bend them
As he went out and in to fetch the cows—
Some boy too far from town to learn baseball,
Whose only play was what he found himself,
Summer or winter, and could play alone.
(28)  One by one he subdued his father's trees
By riding them down over and over again
Until he took the stiffness out of them,
And not one but hung limp, not one was left
For him to conquer. He learned all there was
(33)  To learn about not launching out too soon
And so not carrying the tree away
Clear to the ground. He always kept his poise
To the top branches, climbing carefully
With the same pains you use to fill a cup
(38)  Up to the brim, and even above the brim.
Then he flung outward, feet first, with a swish,
Kicking his way down through the air to the ground.
So was I once myself a swinger of birches.
And so I dream of going back to be.
(43)  It's when I'm weary of considerations,
And life is too much like a pathless wood
Where your face burns and tickles with the cobwebs
Broken across it, and one eye is weeping
From a twig's having lashed across it open.
(48)  I'd like to get away from earth awhile
And then come back to it and begin over.
May no fate willfully misunderstand me
And half grant what I wish and snatch me away
Not to return. Earth's the right place for love:
I don't know where it's likely to go better.

(54) I'd like to go by climbing a birch tree
And climb black branches up a snow-white
trunk
Toward heaven, till the tree could bear no
more,

(57) But dipped its top and set me down again.
That would be good both going and coming
back.
One could do worse than be a swinger of
birches.

Prose: Read the following passage and then write a well-crafted essay analyzing the speaker's reaction to the death of Henry Clerval.

### Excerpt from *Frankenstein*
### by Mary Shelley

(1) I entered the room where the corpse lay, and was led up to the coffin. How can I describe my sensations on beholding it? I feel yet parched with horror, nor can I reflect on that terrible moment without shuddering and agony, that faintly reminds me of the anguish of the recognition. The trial, the presence

(8) of the magistrate and witnesses, passed like a dream from my memory, when I saw the lifeless form of Henry Clerval stretched before me. I gasped for breath; and, throwing myself on the body, I exclaimed, 'Have my murderous machinations deprived you also, my dearest Henry of life? Two I have already destroyed; other victims await their destiny: but you, Clerval, my friend, my benefactor'

(17) The human frame could no longer support the agonizing suffering that I endured, and I was carried out of the room in strong convulsions.

(21) A fever succeeded to this. I lay for two months on the point of death: my ravings, as I afterwards heard, were frightful; I called

(24) myself the murderer of William, of Justine, and of Clerval. Sometimes I entreated my attendants to assist me in the destruction of the fiend by whom I was tormented; and, at others, I felt the fingers of the monster already grasping my neck, and screamed aloud with agony and terror.

(31) Fortunately, as I spoke my native language, Mr. Kirwin alone understood me; but my gestures and bitter cries were sufficient to affright the other witnesses.

(35) Why did I not die? More miserable than man ever was before, why did I not sink into forgetfulness and rest? Death snatches away many blooming children, the only hopes of their doating parents: how many brides and youthful lovers have been one day in the bloom of health and hope, and the next a

(42) prey for worms and the decay of the tomb! Of what materials was I made, that I could thus resist so many shocks, which, like the turning of the wheel, continually renewed the torture?

Open Question: Writer Leo Tolstoy was quoted as saying: "If it is true that there are as many minds as there are heads, then there are as many loves as there are hearts." Novelists and playwrights are famous for creating memorable relationships among their casts of characters. Select a novel or a play in which there "are as many loves as there are hearts." Then write a well-organized essay in which you explain what these relationships consist of and how they represent different kinds of love. Explain how Tolstoy's idea can apply to the work as a whole. Do not merely summarize the plot.

# Answer Key (Practice Test Three)

| | | | | | |
|---|---|---|---|---|---|
| 1. | (C) | 20. | (E) | 39. | (B) |
| 2. | (E) | 21. | (A) | 40. | (A) |
| 3. | (D) | 22. | (A) | 41. | (D) |
| 4. | (D) | 23. | (D) | 42. | (E) |
| 5. | (D) | 24. | (B) | 43. | (B) |
| 6. | (C) | 25. | (C) | 44. | (B) |
| 7. | (E) | 26. | (E) | 45. | (C) |
| 8. | (A) | 27. | (A) | 46. | (C) |
| 9. | (C) | 28. | (E) | 47. | (E) |
| 10. | (C) | 29. | (A) | 48. | (D) |
| 11. | (A) | 30. | (C) | 49. | (A) |
| 12. | (B) | 31. | (B) | 50. | (A) |
| 13. | (B) | 32. | (A) | 51. | (C) |
| 14. | (D) | 33. | (A) | 52. | (D) |
| 15. | (E) | 34. | (A) | 53. | (C) |
| 16. | (E) | 35. | (B) | 54. | (D) |
| 17. | (B) | 36. | (A) | 55. | (E) |
| 18. | (A) | 37. | (A) | | |
| 19. | (C) | 38. | (C) | | |

# eleven

# PRACTICE TEST FOUR

## Section I: One Hour

**This section includes selections from literary works, followed by questions about their form, content, and style. After reading each selection, choose the best answer to each question.**

Questions 1–15. Read the following poem carefully before choosing your answers.

### "Holy Sonnet V"
by John Donne

*(1)* I am a little world made cunningly
    Of elements, and an angelic sprite;
    But black sin hath betray'd to endless night
    My world's both parts, and, O, both parts
       must die.

*(5)* You which beyond that heaven which was
      most high
    Have found new spheres, and of new land
      can write,

Pour new seas in mine eyes, that so I might
Drown my world with my weeping earnestly,
Or wash it if it must be drown'd no more.

*(10)* But O, it must be burnt; alas! the fire
    Of lust and envy burnt it heretofore,
    And made it fouler ; let their flames retire,
    And burn me, O Lord, with a fiery zeal

*(14)* Of Thee and Thy house, which doth in eating
      heal.

1. The first line in the poem is a declaration that:

   (A) The speaker believes he is a microcosm.

   (B) The speaker believes he was fashioned by a deity.

   (C) The speaker suffers from hallucinations.

   (D) The speaker is proud of his heritage.

   (E) The speaker feels complete in his individuality.

2. *Drown'd no more* (line 9) is an allusion to:

   (A) Noah and the flood

   (B) baptism

   (C) purification ceremonies

   (D) discovery

   (E) Jonah and the whale

3. In the third quatrain, the tonal shift moves from _____ to _____.

   (A) pensive to pleading

   (B) guilt to self-aggrandizing

   (C) grief to self-pity

   (D) mourning to destruction

   (E) melancholy to exclamatory

4. What line contains the turn in this sonnet?

   (A) 8

   (B) 9

   (C) 10

   (D) 11

   (E) 12

5. The message of the couplet can best be described as:

   (A) hopeful and confident

   (B) comforting and encouraging

   (C) prayerful and focused

   (D) excited and inspired

   (E) motivating and positive

6. It can be inferred that the speaker is longing to find:

   (A) community

   (B) confession

   (C) forgiveness

   (D) salvation

   (E) redemption

7. The speaker regards the _____ as the center of the *little world*:

   (A) elements

   (B) spirit

   (C) holiness

   (D) soul

   (E) black sin

8. In line 9, *it* refers to:

   (A) *my weeping*

   (B) *my world*

   (C) *new seas*

   (D) *that heaven*

   (E) *mine eye*

9. The main metaphor in the poem concentrates on:

   (A) water

   (B) fire

   (C) drowning

   (D) guilt

   (E) worldliness

10. When he references *drown[ing his] world* in lines 8–10, the speaker feels

    (A) overwhelming self-pity

    (B) immense loneliness

    (C) ridden with guilt

    (D) a lack of self-worth

    (E) an extreme sense of duty

11. The central theme of the poem is:

    (A) Sin and purity exist in duality and conflict.

    (B) Personal redemption requires specific, necessary steps.

    (C) Good and evil must coexist to provide balance in the world.

    (D) Drastic guilt can lead to extreme bargaining.

    (E) confession is essential to renewal.

12. The author creates his message primarily through:

    (A) metaphor

    (B) symbolism

    (C) allegory

    (D) paradox

    (E) meter

13. The word *fouler* in line 12 is closest in meaning to:

(A) repugnant

(B) nefarious

(C) bscene

(D) putrid

(E) entangled

14. The poem contains all of the following except:

(A) metaphor

(B) personification

(C) hyperbole

(D) imagery

(E) anastrophe

Questions 15–25. Read the poem on the next page carefully before choosing your answers.

## "Your Riches Taught Me Poverty"
### by Emily Dickinson

(1) Your Riches—taught me—Poverty.
Myself—a Millionaire
In little Wealths, as Girls could boast
Till broad as Buenos Ayre—

(5) You drifted your Dominions—
A Different Peru—
And I esteemed All Poverty
For Life's Estate with you—

(9) Of Mines, I little know—myself—
But just the names, of Gems—
The Colors of the Commonest—
And scarce of Diadems—

(13) So much, that did I meet the Queen—
Her Glory I should know—
But this, must be a different Wealth—
To miss it—beggars so—

(17) I'm sure 'tis India—all Day—
To those who look on You—
Without a stint—without a blame,
Might I—but be the Jew—

(21) I'm sure it is Golconda—
Beyond my power to deem—
To have a smile for Mine—each Day,
How better, than a Gem!

(25) At least, it solaces to know
That there exists—a Gold—
Altho' I prove it, just in time
Its distance—to behold—

(29) Its far—far Treasure to surmise—
And estimate the Pearl—
That slipped my simple fingers through—
While just a Girl at School.

15. In the first stanza, the speaker asserts:

(A) that she was unaware of her status until she encountered *you*

(B) that she now has a full understanding of poverty

(C) that she views herself as a millionaire

(D) that she finds *your riches* inadequate

(E) that she admires *your riches*

16. The topic of the poem could best be described as:

(A) the destructive influence of other people

(B) the vast world outside the self

(C) the riches of human relationships

(D) the unimportance of material wealth

(E) the lessons learned from poverty

17. One possible theme from the poem would be:

(A) The common person is not capable of aspiring to true wealth.

(B) We find the greatest treasure in the small pleasures of life.

(C) The wealthy cannot comprehend wealth that is not material.

(D) The poor possess life's greatest riches.

(E) Observe the meek to discover life's true blessings.

GO ON

18. The word *diadems* (line 12) most likely refers to:

    (A)  crowns

    (B)  power

    (C)  royalty

    (D)  adorning

    (E)  tiaras

19. When the speaker indicates the things she does not know about in line 9, it indicates:

    (A)  the speaker's age

    (B)  the speaker's humility

    (C)  that the speaker is naïve

    (D)  the speaker's ability to laugh at herself

    (E)  the speaker's desire for wealth

20. The poem contains all of the following literary devices except:

    (A)  anaphora

    (B)  paradox

    (C)  simile

    (D)  allusion

    (E)  irony

21. What does the speaker accomplish in using dashes?

    (A)  fluidity of thought

    (B)  interruption of thought

    (C)  additional linguistic meaning

    (D)  stability

    (E)  rhythm

22. The lines *You drifted your Dominions—/A Different Peru—* (lines 5–6) suggest that the person being addressed by the speaker:

    (A)  recently moved far away from the speaker

    (B)  doesn't want to be friends with the speaker anymore

    (C)  is not impressed with the speaker's wealth

    (D)  wants something different from what the speaker valued as a girl

    (E)  have given away her wealth in order to live a life of poverty

23. The line *To have a smile for Mine—each Day,/How better, than a Gem!* (lines 23–24) indicate that the speaker:

    (A)  has no concept of material wealth

    (B)  possesses contentment with her life

    (C)  finds joy in the rich implications of simplicity

    (D)  has not received a proper education

    (E)  focuses on the proper priorities

24. The word *surmise* on line 29 most likely means:

    (A)  suppose

    (B)  estimate

    (C)  infer

    (D)  conjecture

    (E)  imply

25. India most likely stands for:

    (A)  any faraway destination

    (B)  the homeland of the addressee

    (C)  a representation of the poem's paradox

    (D)  personal prohibition

    (E)  opulence and luxury

Questions 26–39. Read the following passage carefully before choosing your answers.

## Excerpt from *Don Quixote*
### by Miguel de Cervantes

(1) These preliminaries settled, he did not care to put off any longer the execution of his design, urged on to it by the thought of all the world was losing by his delay, seeing what wrongs he intended to right, grievances to redress, injustices to repair, abuses to remove, and duties to discharge. So, without giving

(8) notice of his intention to anyone, and without anybody seeing him, one morning before the dawning of the day (which was one of the hottest of the month of July) he donned his suit of armour, mounted Rocinante with his patched-up helmet on, braced his buckler, took his lance, and by the back door of the yard sallied forth upon the plain in

(16) the highest contentment and satisfaction at seeing with what ease he had made a beginning with his grand purpose. But scarcely did he find himself upon the open plain, when a terrible thought struck him, one all but enough to make him abandon the enterprise at the very outset. It occurred to him that he had not been dubbed a knight,

(24) and that according to the law of chivalry he neither could nor ought to bear arms against any knight; and that even if he had been, still he ought, as a novice knight, to wear white armour, without a device upon the shield until by his prowess he had earned one. These reflections made him waver in his purpose, but his craze being stronger than

(32) any reasoning, he made up his mind to have himself dubbed a knight by the first one he came across, following the example of others in the same case, as he had read in the books that brought him to this pass. As for white armor, he resolved, on the first opportunity, to scour his until it was whiter than an ermine; and so comforting himself he pursued his way, taking that which his horse chose, for in

(41) this he believed lay the essence of adventures. Thus setting out, our new-fledged adventurer paced along, talking to himself and saying, "Who knows but that in time to come, when the veracious history of my famous deeds is made known, the sage who writes it, when he has to set forth my first sally in the early morning, will do it after this fashion? 'Scarce

(49) had the rubicund Apollo spread o'er the face of the broad spacious earth the golden threads of his bright hair, scarce had the little birds of painted plumage attuned their notes to hail with dulcet and mellifluous harmony the coming of the rosy Dawn, that, deserting the soft couch of her jealous spouse, was appearing to mortals at the gates and balconies of the Manchegan horizon,

(57) when the renowned knight Don Quixote of La Mancha, quitting the lazy down, mounted his celebrated steed Rocinante and began to traverse the ancient and famous Campo de Montiel;'" which in fact he was actually traversing. "Happy the age, happy the time," he continued, "in which shall be made known

(65) my deeds of fame, worthy to be molded in brass, carved in marble, limned in pictures, for a memorial for ever. And thou, O sage magician, whoever thou art, to whom it shall fall to be the chronicler of this wondrous history, forget not, I entreat thee, my good Rocinante, the constant companion of my ways and wanderings." Presently he broke

(73) out again, as if he were love-stricken in earnest, "O Princess Dulcinea, lady of this captive heart, a grievous wrong hast thou done me to drive me forth with scorn, and with inexorable obduracy banish me from the presence of thy beauty. O lady, deign to hold in remembrance this heart, thy vassal, that thus in anguish pines for love of thee."

GO ON

26. Lines 48–63 use all of the following literary devices except:

   (A) hyperbole

   (B) alliteration

   (C) parallel structure

   (D) imagery

   (E) anaphora

27. What is the *terrible thought* Don Quixote refers to in line 20?

   (A) that someone would find out the truth about his plan

   (B) his not knowing where he was going

   (C) the wrongs that his lady had done him

   (D) his status not being quite legitimate

   (E) his ambitions being too great

28. The genre of the narrative most closely resembles:

   (A) adventure

   (B) epic

   (C) tragedy

   (D) comedy

   (E) farce

29. According to Don Quixote's chivalric code, a knight is not meant to do any of the following except:

   (A) travel directly and purposefully

   (B) speak plainly and succinctly

   (C) maintain a supercilious attitude about himself

   (D) avoid romantic entanglement

   (E) disregard unreasonable rules

30. The word *veracious* in line 24 most likely means:

   (A) accurate

   (B) mendacious

   (C) loquacious

   (D) avid

   (E) historical

31. It is clear that the author's attitude towards Don Quixote is:

   (A) magnanimous

   (B) compassionate

   (C) sympathetic

   (D) sardonic

   (E) idealistic

32. What does the speaker say is stronger than Don Quixote's reasoning?

   (A) his abilities

   (B) his passion

   (C) his craze

   (D) his physical strength

   (E) his sensitivities

33. The word *inexorable* in line 77 means:

   (A) relentless

   (B) unyielding

   (C) soft

   (D) flexible

   (E) inevitable

34. The author reveals much about Don Quixote through all of the following except:

   (A) interior thought

   (B) interaction with others

   (C) physical description

   (D) behaviors

   (E) verbal dialogue

35. The speaker's point of view is:

   (A) first-person limited

   (B) first-person omniscient

   (C) second person

   (D) third-person limited

   (E) third-person omniscient

36. The author mainly describes the sunrise through the use of:

(A) allegory

(B) symbolism

(C) sound imagery

(D) visual imagery

(E) personification

37. Based on lines 63–72, it is clear that Don Quixote:

(A) suffers from delusional behaviors

(B) compensates for a low self-esteem

(C) motivates himself to determine his goals

(D) possesses a skewed sense of self

(E) plans for great success and fame in the future

38. The word *rubicund* (line 49) means:

(A) round

(B) healthy

(C) red

(D) pale

(E) weak

39. It is clear by the ending words of Don Quixote in this passage that he views Dulcinea as:

(A) a perfect lady-in-waiting on whom to practice his chivalric code

(B) a possible match for marriage

(C) an honorable woman whom he must address with utmost respect

(D) someone of whom he feels unworthy

(E) someone who can grant him authentic knighthood

Questions 40–55. Read the following passage carefully before choosing your answers.

### Excerpt from *A Tale of Two Cities*
by Charles Dickens

*(1)* It was the best of times, it was the worst of times, it was the age of wisdom, it was the age of foolishness, it was the epoch of belief, it was the epoch of incredulity, it was the season of Light, it was the season of Darkness, it was the spring of hope, it was the winter of despair, we had everything before us, we had *(8)* nothing before us, we were all going direct to Heaven, we were all going direct the other way—in short, the period was so far like the present period, that some of its noisiest authorities insisted on its being received, for good or for evil, in the superlative degree of comparison only.

*(15)* There were a king with a large jaw and a queen with a plain face, on the throne of England; there were a king with a large jaw and a queen with a fair face, on the throne of France. In both countries it was clearer than crystal to the lords of the State preserves of loaves and fishes, that things in general were settled for ever.

*(23)* It was the year of Our Lord one thousand seven hundred and seventy-five. Spiritual

*(25)* revelations were conceded to England at that favoured period, as at this. Mrs. Southcott had recently attained her five-and-twentieth blessed birthday, of whom a prophetic private in the Life Guards had heralded the sublime appearance by announcing that arrangements were made for the swallowing up of London *(32)* and Westminster. Even the Cock-lane ghost had been laid only a round dozen of years, after rapping out its messages, as the spirits of this very year last past (supernaturally deficient in originality) rapped out theirs. Mere messages in the earthly order of events had lately come to the English Crown and *(39)* People, from a congress of British subjects in America: which, strange to relate, have proved more important to the human race than any communications yet received through any of the chickens of the Cock-lane brood.

*(45)* France, less favoured on the whole as to matters spiritual than her sister of the shield and trident, rolled with exceeding smoothness down hill, making paper money

(49) and spending it. Under the guidance of her Christian pastors, she entertained herself, besides, with such humane achievements as sentencing a youth to have his hands cut off, his tongue torn out with pincers, and his body burned alive, because he had not kneeled down in the rain to do honour to a dirty procession of monks which passed

(57) within his view, at a distance of some fifty or sixty yards. It is likely enough that, rooted in the woods of France and Norway, there were growing trees, when that sufferer was put to death, already marked by the Woodman, Fate, to come down and be sawn into boards, to make a certain movable framework

(64) with a sack and a knife in it, terrible in history. It is likely enough that in the rough outhouses of some tillers of the heavy lands adjacent to Paris, there were sheltered from the weather that very day, rude carts, bespattered with rustic mire, snuffed about by pigs, and roosted in by poultry, which

(71) the Farmer, Death, had already set apart to be his tumbrils of the Revolution. But that Woodman and that Farmer, though they work unceasingly, work silently, and no one heard them as they went about with muffled tread: the rather, forasmuch as to entertain any suspicion that they were awake, was to be atheistical and traitorous.

(79) In England, there was scarcely an amount of order and protection to justify much national boasting. Daring burglaries by armed men, and highway robberies, took place in the capital itself every night; families were publicly cautioned not to go out of town without removing their furniture to upholsterers' warehouses for security;

(87) the highwayman in the dark was a City tradesman in the light, and, being recognised and challenged by his fellow-tradesman whom he stopped in his character of "the Captain," gallantly shot him through the head and rode away; the mall was waylaid by seven robbers, and the guard shot three dead, and then got shot dead himself by the

(95) other four, "in consequence of the failure of his ammunition:" after which the mall was robbed in peace; that magnificent potentate, the Lord Mayor of London, was made to stand and deliver on Turnham Green, by one highwayman, who despoiled the illustrious creature in sight of all his retinue; prisoners in London gaols fought battles

(103) with their turnkeys, and the majesty of the law fired blunderbusses in among them, loaded with rounds of shot and ball; thieves snipped off diamond crosses from the necks of noble lords at Court drawing-rooms; musketeers went into St. Giles's, to search for contraband goods, and the mob fired on the musketeers, and the musketeers fired

(111) on the mob, and nobody thought any of these occurrences much out of the common way. In the midst of them, the hangman, ever busy and ever worse than useless, was in constant requisition; now, stringing up long rows of miscellaneous criminals; now, hanging a housebreaker on Saturday who had been taken on Tuesday; now, burning

(119) people in the hand at Newgate by the dozen, and now burning pamphlets at the door of Westminster Hall; to-day, taking the life of an atrocious murderer, and to-morrow of a wretched pilferer who had robbed a farmer's boy of sixpence.

40. The opening sentence of the passage relies on primarily which literary device?

(A) antithesis

(B) symbolism

(C) metaphor

(D) alliteration

(E) hyperbole

41. The purpose of this particular opening statement is to:

(A) dramatize the polarity of the two settings

(B) introduce the reader to the novel

(C) engage the reader in a political conversation

(D) draw the reader's attention to historical events

(E) compel the reader to read further

42. The two cities serve as a(n):

    (A) paradox

    (B) foil

    (C) allegory

    (D) symbol

    (E) character

43. It can be inferred that the trouble in this passage derives from:

    (A) London

    (B) the stagnation of the two cities

    (C) Paris

    (D) the American revolution

    (E) the setting at large

44. Lines 58–72 contain examples of:

    (A) personification

    (B) allegory

    (C) antithesis

    (D) anaphora

    (E) parallel structure

45. The purpose of this passage is to introduce:

    (A) plot

    (B) characters

    (D) setting

    (D) narrator

    (E) tone

46. From the beginning of the fourth paragraph (lines 45-58) it can be inferred that the speaker believes France's religious leaders to be:

    (A) shameful

    (B) admirable

    (C) greedy

    (D) violent

    (E) wealthy

47. The reader can infer from this passage that a prominent structural motif for the remainder of the novel will be:

    (A) the journey of escape

    (B) the duplicity of people

    (C) the corruption of power

    (D) oppression of the poor

    (E) the inward struggle of the whole

48. The allusion in line 21 refers to an event from:

    (A) American history

    (B) European history

    (C) the Bible

    (D) the Talmud

    (E) Shakespeare's works

49. The primary tone in lines 49–58 is one of:

    (A) anger and despair

    (B) pragmatism and stoicism

    (C) melancholy and wistful

    (D) realistic and despondent

    (E) pessimistic and detrimental

50. The final stanza indicates that:

    (A) Death is on the rampage in both cities.

    (B) Crime has become the norm.

    (C) People are growing desensitized to violence.

    (D) London is far worse a city than Paris.

    (E) The denizens expect the situation to stay at the status quo.

51. The Woodman represents:

    (A) violence

    (B) death

    (C) farming

    (D) fate

    (E) crime

GO ON

52. The symbol that most likely represents the Farmer is the:

(A) guillotine

(B) gallows

(C) tumbrils

(D) scythe

(E) stake

53. The author describes the events of the time by employing mainly:

(A) sound imagery

(B) visual imagery

(C) details

(D) diction

(E) syntax

54. The writer's comments about English traditions in line 23–32 can best be described as:

(A) allegory

(B) historical fiction

(C) Gothic fiction

(D) farce

(E) satire

55. The passage is told from the _____ point of view.

(A) first person limited

(B) first person omniscient

(C) second person

(D) third person limited

(E) third person omniscient

# Section II: One Hour

**Directions: This section includes selections from literary works, followed by questions that will ask you to address their form, content, and style. After reading each selection, craft a well-written essay that responds to the question.**

Poetry: Read the following poem carefully. Then write a well-organized essay in which you explain how formal elements such as structure, syntax, diction, and imagery reveal the speaker's response to death.

### "Death's Chill Between"
by Christina Georgina Rossetti

(1)  Chide not; let me breathe a little,
     For I shall not mourn him long;
     Though the life-cord was so brittle,
     The love-cord was very strong.
     I would wake a little space
     Till I find a sleeping-place.

(7)  You can go,—I shall not weep;
     You can go unto your rest.
     My heart-ache is all too deep,
     And too sore my throbbing breast.
     Can sobs be, or angry tears,
     Where are neither hopes nor fears?

(13)  Though with you I am alone
     And must be so everywhere,
     I will make no useless moan,—
     None shall say 'She could not bear:'
     While life lasts I will be strong,—
     But I shall not struggle long.

(19)  Listen, listen! Everywhere
     A low voice is calling me,
     And a step is on the stair,

And one comes ye do not see,
Listen, listen! Evermore
A dim hand knocks at the door.

(25)  Hear me; he is come again,—
     My own dearest is come back.
     Bring him in from the cold rain;
     Bring wine, and let nothing lack.
     Thou and I will rest together,
     Love, until the sunny weather.

(31)  I will shelter thee from harm,—
     Hide thee from all heaviness.
     Come to me, and keep thee warm
     By my side in quietness.
     I will lull thee to thy sleep
     With sweet songs:—we will not weep.

(37)  Who hath talked of weeping?—Yet
     There is something at my heart,
     Gnawing, I would fain forget,
     And an aching and a smart.
     —Ah! my mother, 'tis in vain,
     For he is not come again.

GO ON

Prose: Read the following passage and write a well-organized essay in which you address the role of landscape in the passage.

## Excerpt from *Cry, the Beloved Country*
### Alan Paton

(1) There is a lovely road that runs from Ixopo into the hills. These hills are grass-covered and rolling, and they are lovely beyond any singing of it. The road climbs seven miles into them, to Carisbrooke; and from there, if there is no mist, you look down on one of the fairest valleys of Africa. About you

(8) there is grass and bracken and you may hear the forlorn crying of the titihoya, one of the birds of the veld. Below you is the valley of the Umzimkulu, on its journey from the Drakensberg to the sea; and beyond and behind the river, great hill after great hill; and beyond and behind them, the mountains of Ingeli and East Griqualand.

(16) The grass is rich and matted, you cannot see the soil. It holds the rain and the mist, and they seep into the ground, feeding the streams in every kloof. It is well tended, and not too many cattle feed upon it; not too

(21) many fires burn it, laying bare the soil. Stand unshod upon it, for the ground is holy, being even as it came from the Creator. Keep it, guard it, care for it, for it keeps men, guards men, cares for men. Destroy it and man is

(26) destroyed. Where you stand the grass is rich and matted, you cannot see the soil. But the rich green hills break down. They fall to the valley below, and falling, change their nature. For they grow red and bare; they cannot hold the rain and mist, and the streams are

(32) dry in the kloofs. Too many cattle feed upon the grass, and too many fires have burned it. Stand shod upon it, for it is coarse and sharp, and the stones cut under the feet. It is not kept, or guarded, or cared for, it no longer keeps men, guards men, cares for men. The titihoya does not cry here any more.

(39) The great red hills stand desolate, and the earth has torn away like flesh. The lightning flashes over them, the clouds pour down upon them, the dead streams come to life, full of the red blood of the earth. Down in the

(44) valleys women scratch the soil that is left, and the maize hardly reaches the height of a man. They are valleys of old men and old women, of mothers and children. The men are away, the young men and the girls are away. The soil cannot keep them any more.

Open Question: A recurring theme in literature is the classic war between entrapment and freedom. Choose a literary work in which a character becomes free from his or her state of physical or mental imprisonment. In a well-written essay, clearly demonstrate the effects of entrapment and freedom upon the character and its significance to the work.

## Answer Key (Practice Test Four)

| | | | | | |
|---|---|---|---|---|---|
| 1. | (A) | 20. | (A) | 39. | (A) |
| 2. | (A) | 21. | (A) | 40. | (E) |
| 3. | (D) | 22. | (D) | 41. | (A) |
| 4. | (C) | 23. | (C) | 42. | (B) |
| 5. | (A) | 24. | (D) | 43. | (B) |
| 6. | (E) | 25. | (E) | 44. | (A) |
| 7. | (D) | 26. | (A) | 45. | (C) |
| 8. | (B) | 27. | (D) | 46. | (E) |
| 9. | (B) | 28. | (E) | 47. | (B) |
| 10. | (C) | 29. | (C) | 48. | (C) |
| 11. | (A) | 30. | (A) | 49. | (A) |
| 12. | (D) | 31. | (A) | 50. | (A) |
| 13. | (B) | 32. | (C) | 51. | (D) |
| 14. | (B) | 33. | (B) | 52. | (C) |
| 15. | (A) | 34. | (B) | 53. | (B) |
| 16. | (C) | 35. | (B) | 54. | (E) |
| 17. | (B) | 36. | (E) | 55. | (B) |
| 18. | (A) | 37. | (D) | | |
| 19. | (C) | 38. | (C) | | |